SPECTRUM®

Common Core
Language Arts and Math

Grade 3

Published by Spectrum®
An imprint of Carson-Dellosa Publishing LLC
Greensboro, North Carolina

Spectrum®
An imprint of Carson-Dellosa Publishing LLC
P.O. Box 35665
Greensboro, NC 27425 USA

ISBN 978-1-4838-0451-4

01-031141151

Table of Contents

Introduction to the Common Core State Standards
Grade 3

Why Are Common Core State Standards Important for My Child?

The Common Core State Standards are a set of guidelines that outline what children are expected to learn at school. Most U.S. states have voluntarily adopted the standards. Teachers, principals, and administrators in these states use the standards as a blueprint for classroom lessons, district curriculum, and statewide tests. The standards were developed by a state-led collaboration between the Council of Chief State School Officers (CCSSO) and the National Governors Association (NGA).

The Common Core Standards set high expectations for your child's learning. They are up-to-date with 21st century technology and draw on the best practices of excellent schools around the world. They focus on important skills in reading, language arts, and math. Common Core State Standards aim to ensure that your child will be college and career ready by the end of high school and able to compete in our global world.

What Are the Common Core State Standards for My Third Grade Student?

Common Core State Standards for your third grader are designed to build a solid foundation for reading, literacy, and mathematical understanding. On practice pages in this book, you will find references to specific Common Core Standards that teachers will expect your child to know by the end of the year. Completing activities on these pages will help your child master essential skills for success in third grade.

A Sample of Common Core English Language Arts Skills for Grade 3

- Determine the meaning of an unknown word by examining the context surrounding it.
- Know the meaning of common prefixes and suffixes.
- Write opinion pieces, informative texts, and stories with strong introductions and conclusions.
- Use dialogue to make writing more interesting.
- Explain the functions of nouns, pronouns, verbs, adjectives, and adverbs.
- Use correct subject-verb agreement when writing sentences.

A Sample of Common Core Math Skills for Grade 3

- Multiply and divide within 100.
- Solve two-step word problems using addition, subtraction, multiplication, and division.
- Round numbers to the nearest ten and hundred.
- Compare equivalent fractions.
- Interpret data on bar graphs, pictographs, and line plots.
- Find the perimeter and area of shapes.

How to Use This Book

In this book, you will find a complete **Common Core State Standards Overview** for third grade English Language Arts (pages 6–9) and Math (pages 64–67). Read these pages to learn more about the Common Core Standards and what you can expect your child to learn at school this year.

Then, choose **Practice Pages** that best address your child's needs for building skills that meet specific standards. Help your child complete practice pages and check the answers.

At the bottom of each practice page, you will find a **Helping at Home** tip that provides fun and creative ideas for additional practice with the skill at home.

Common Core State Standards for English Language Arts*

The following parent-friendly explanations of third grade Common Core English language arts standards are provided to help you understand what your child will learn in school this year. Practice pages listed will help your child master each skill.

Complete Common Core State Standards may be found here: www.corestandards.org.

RL/RI.3 Reading Standards for Literature and Informational Text

Key Ideas and Details
(Standards RL.3.1, RL.3.2, RL.3.3, RI.3.1, RI.3.2, RI.3.3)

After reading a story or information article, your child will answer questions about the main idea of the text, referring to key details in the text to support his or her answers.
• **Practice pages: 10, 11, 14–21, 26–27**

Your child will describe characters in stories and explain how each character's actions contribute to the overall plot. • **Practice pages: 10, 11, 14, 15, 24, 25**

Your child will describe the relationship between ideas or steps in an information article.
• **Practice pages: 24–27**

Craft and Structure
(Standards: RL.3.4, RL.3.6, RI.3.4)

Your child will identify unfamiliar words and phrases in a text and use strategies, such as context clues, to find the meanings of the words. • **Practice pages: 10–21, 24, 25**

When reading a text, your child will be able to separate his or her point of view from that of the narrator, characters, or author. • **Practice pages: 12, 13**

Integration of Knowledge and Ideas
(Standards: RI.3.7, RI.3.8)

Your child will connect visual aids, such as maps or photographs, with details in a text to better understand the information presented in the text. • **Practice pages: 20–25**

Your child will decide whether sentences and paragraphs in a text are connected by comparison and contrast, cause and effect, sequencing, etc. • **Practice pages: 22, 23**

RF.3 Reading Standards: Foundational Skills

Phonics and Word Recognition
(Standards: RF.3.3a, RF.3.3b, RF.3.3c)

Your child will learn the meaning and usage of prefixes such as micro– (example: microchip) and suffixes such as –less (example: ageless). • **Practice pages: 28–30**

Your child will identify base words and suffixes that change a word's meaning. • **Practice page: 29**

Your child will recognize the number of syllables in a word and use context clues to decode multi-syllable words. • **Practice pages: 31–35**

W.3 Writing Standards

Text Types and Purposes
(Standards: W.3.1, W.3.2, W.3.3)

Your child will write to persuade readers. • **Practice page: 36**

Your child will write to provide information about a topic. • **Practice pages: 37, 38**

Your child will write stories that include dialogue and a clear sequence of events. • **Practice pages: 39–44**

Production and Distribution of Writing
(Standards: W.3.4, W.3.5)

When writing, your child will think about the specific task, purpose, and audience and organize ideas in the writing to fit. • **Practice pages: 45, 46**

Your child will improve his or her writing by planning, writing, revising, and editing. • **Practice page: 47**

Research to Build and Present Knowledge
(Standards: W.3.7, W.3.8)

Your child will gather information and take notes from books, magazines, or credible Web resources to write short research reports. • **Practice page: 48**

Common Core State Standards for English Language Arts*

L.3 Language Standards

Conventions of Standard English
(Standards: L.3.1a, L.3.1b, L.3.1c, L.3.1d, L.3.1e, L.3.1f,
L.3.1g, L.3.1h, L.3.1i, L.3.2c, L.3.2d, L.3.2f)

Your child will recognize linking verbs such as is and action verbs such as swim. Your child will learn about irregular past tense verbs such as drew. • **Practice pages: 49, 57**

Your child will learn that an adjective describes a noun. • **Practice page: 50**

Your child will recognize adverbs in sentences and identify the verbs they modify.
• **Practice page: 51**

Your child will use pronouns, such as him or it, to replace nouns in a sentence.
• **Practice page: 53**

Your child will use singular and plural nouns such as boy and boys. • **Practice page: 54**

Your child will understand the difference between concrete nouns, such as dog, and abstract nouns, such as kindness. • **Practice page: 55**

Your child will use the present, past, and future tenses correctly when writing sentences such as I talk, I talked, and I will talk. • **Practice page: 56**

Your child will learn that a singular subject takes a singular verb (example: This park has a bench) and a plural subject takes a plural verb (example: These parks have trails).
• **Practice page: 61**

Your child will add –er and –est to adjectives and adverbs, such as smarter and hardest, to compare two or more nouns or actions. • **Practice pages: 52, 58**

Your child will connect words, phrases, clauses, and sentences with coordinating conjunctions, such as and, but, or or. • **Practice page: 59**

Your child will use quotation marks and commas to indicate who is speaking.
• **Practice page: 60**

Your child will write possessive nouns to show ownership, such as the girl's bag or the students' test. • **Practice pages: 18, 19, 62**

Your child will combine sentences using words such as after or because. • **Practice page: 27**

Your child will use an understanding of word parts, syllables, and spelling patterns to help write words. • **Practice pages: 12, 13**

Knowledge of Language
(Standard: L.3.3a)

Your child will choose words and phrases to make writing more specific and interesting.
• **Practice page: 63**

Vocabulary Acquisition and Use
(Standards: L.3.4, L.3.5a)

Your child will learn strategies for finding the meaning of an unknown word. He or she will look for context clues in surrounding text; think about the meaning of any root words, prefixes, or suffixes; or look up the word in a dictionary. • **Practice pages: 17, 22, 23, 26, 27, 33–35**

Your child will understand that some words and phrases, such as butterflies in your stomach, have nonliteral meanings. • **Practice pages: 14–17**

Understanding a Text

Read the story.

An Ordinary Day

Rachel stepped off the school bus with a sad look on her face. Her mother waited for her by the mailbox.

"Hey, why the **long face**?" her mother asked.

"Today was boring," Rachel replied. "There were no tests, nothing **special** for lunch, no extra recesses, no special programs. It was just an ordinary day."

"But the ordinary days make the exciting days seem exciting," Rachel's mother explained. "If we had no ordinary days, we might never notice the exciting days."

Rachel thought about what her mother had said. Maybe ordinary days were as special as exciting days.

Annika

Understanding a Text

Answer the questions using the story on page 10.

1. Why was Rachel sad?
   A. She got a bad grade on a test.
   B. She had an argument with her friend.
   C. She had an ordinary day.

2. What did Rachel learn?
   A. Ordinary days make exciting days more exciting.
   B. Occasionally, everyone has a bad day.
   C. Her mother has bad days, too.

3. Number the events from least exciting (1) to most exciting (6).

   _2_ spelling test

   _1_ hamburger at lunch

   _6_ birthday party

   _5_ special school program

   _3_ library day

   _4_ extra recess

4. What is the opposite of *special*? ___unspecial___

5. What does the phrase *long face* mean?
   A. sad look
   B. happy look
   C. excited look

Helping at Home

Discuss the story's lesson with your child. Then, have him or her describe a recent ordinary day and a recent special day. Compare the two days and ask your child if he or she agrees with the lesson in this story.

Word Meaning and Point of View

Read the poem.

The County Fair

I love to go to the county fair.
I love the noises and the smells in the air.

The people, the animals, and the food
All create a festive mood.

You can hear the animals in the shed
Calling out loudly to be fed.

The barkers holler, "Come on and play,
I bet you're feeling lucky today."

The Ferris wheel spins high in the sky.
It makes me feel like I can fly.

The rides are fast and so exciting,
Especially the one they call Blue Lightning.

Hot dogs, drinks, and cotton candy,
The **vendors** sell and make so dandy.

I love to go to the county fair.
I love the fun and excitement there.

Word Meaning and Point of View

Answer the questions using the poem on page 12.

1. How does the author feel about the county fair?
   A. The author enjoys the county fair.
   B. The author thinks the county fair is boring.
   C. The author thinks the county fair is overwhelming.

2. Tell how you and the author feel the same and differently about a county fair.

   I like the food

3. Use the poem to think about a county fair.

   A. Write two things that you can see. _People & food_

   B. Write two things that you can hear. _animals & people talking_

   C. Write two things that you can smell. _air & food_

   D. Write two things that you can touch. _food & animals_

   E. Write two things that you can taste. _fish & corn drink_

4. What does the word *vendor* mean?
   A. a person who sells things
   B. a person who runs the rides
   C. a person who manages the county fair

Write a word from the poem that rhymes with each word listed. Then, think of another word that rhymes with it.

5. fair _____   _____

6. shed _____   _____

7. sky _____   _____

8. play _____   _____

Helping at Home

Ask your child what visiting a fair would be like for an animal. What kind of sights, sounds, and smells would the animal notice? Have your child write a short poem from an animal's point of view and compare it to the poem on page 12.

Characters and Events

Read the story.

Grandpa Remembers

My grandpa lived just down the lane and around the corner from my family. I loved to go to his house and spend time with him. He taught me how to fish and play checkers. In the wintertime, we would sit by the fire and play games. In the summertime, we would go for long walks. **Time** always **flew** when I was with my grandpa. My favorite times with Grandpa were the "remembering" times. Grandpa loved to tell stories about how things used to be. Grandpa always said he hoped he didn't **talk my ear off**. But, I loved to listen to Grandpa's stories.

"One cold winter's day, when I wasn't much older than you," Grandpa began, "I begged to go with my dad to harvest a crop of ice blocks."

"A crop of ice blocks?" I interrupted. "You're **pulling my leg**, Grandpa."

"I am not pulling your leg," stated Grandpa. "Where was I? Oh, yes. When I was young, people didn't have refrigerators like they do now. Gathering ice blocks was the only way to keep foods cold through the spring and summer."

"I helped my dad get the tractor and wagon hooked up," Grandpa continued. "Then, we drove down to the river. When we got there, Dad tested the ice. 'Looks like we found an excellent stretch of ice,' he'd say. Then, he took the logging saw. A logging saw is a long saw with handles at each end. I watched as my dad put the saw in the water. Pushing and then pulling, he cut a long slab of ice. Then, I helped him move the slab up the bank to the wagon. He let me hold onto one end of the saw, and we worked together to cut the slab into square blocks. Then, my dad used large ice tongs to put the blocks of ice on the wagon. When the ice blocks were loaded, we

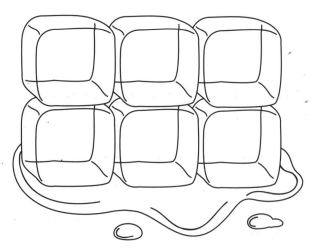

hit the road** and headed to the ice shed. The ice shed had three or four inches of sawdust on the floor. We put the blocks on top of the sawdust. Then, we packed more sawdust around the blocks. We would store all of our food that needed to stay cold inside the ice shed."

The "remembering" times were some of my favorite times with my grandpa. It was fun to **shoot the breeze** with him and learn about how things were when he was my age. I will always remember our "remembering" times. Someday, I would like to have "remembering times" with my grandchildren.

Characters and Events

Answer the questions using the story on page 14.

1. What are "remembering" times?

   A. telling stories of long ago

   B. remembering what needs to be done

   C. listening and trying to remember details of a story

2. Number the sentences as they happened in Grandpa's story.

   _____ We put the blocks of ice in the ice shed.

   _____ We went down to the river.

   _____ He cut a slab of ice.

   _____ We loaded the blocks of ice onto the wagon.

   _____ We worked together to cut the slab into square blocks.

3. How do you think the author of the story feels about his grandpa?

   A. loves him   B. feels sorry for him   C. thinks he's a bit boring

4. Draw a line between each saying and its meaning.

   pulling my leg   talk too much

   hit the road   go or leave

   talk my ear off   talk about nothing in particular

   shoot the breeze   time passed quickly

   time flew   teasing me

When a word ends with a vowel and a consonant, the consonant is usually doubled before adding *-ed* or *-ing*. Double the last consonant of the word in parentheses. Then, add *-ed* or *-ing* and write the word on the blank.

5. I _____ to go harvest a crop of ice. (beg)

6. A _____ saw has handles at each end. (log)

Details in a Text

Read the poem.

Heroes

Heroes are people like you and me,
Who choose to act selflessly.

Heroes give all they have, then give some more.
Heroes take action when action's called for.

Heroes pick themselves up when they make mistakes.
Heroes keep trying. They've got what it takes.

Heroes are willing to give their all.
They stop, look, and listen, then answer the call.

We look to heroes to show us the way,
To go the extra mile, to seize the day.

So, be kind and helpful wherever you go.
For someone may look to you as a hero.

Details in a Text

Answer the questions using the poem on page 16.

1. Write an **X** if the sentence describes a hero.

_____ Heroes choose to act selflessly.

_____ Heroes give it their all.

_____ Heroes make a lot of money.

_____ Heroes keep trying.

_____ Heroes are very tall.

_____ Heroes go the extra mile.

2. Why should you be kind and helpful?
   A. because someone may think you are a hero
   B. because your mom wants you to be
   C. because other people will be kind to you

3. Who is your hero? Write two things that make this person a hero.

_____

_____

_____

4. What does *Heroes pick themselves up when they make mistakes* mean?
   A. They stand up when they fall down.
   B. They try again when they make a mistake.
   C. They always do things right.

5. "Give it their all," "Go the extra mile," and "Seize the day" are all sayings that mean the same thing. What do they mean?
   A. be a good friend
   B. never give up
   C. believe in yourself

Main Ideas

Read the passage.

Heroes of Long Ago

Knights were heroes of long ago. They were soldiers in Europe from about 900 to 1500 A.D. Knights lived before the time of guns. They fought in hand-to-hand combat. Knights served their king. They had a set of rules, also called a **code of conduct**, to obey.

Knights wore heavy suits called *armor*. The armor weighed about 55 pounds (25 kg). The armor protected the knight during battle. For a knight, the armor was a symbol that stood for honor, valor, and chivalry. Because of this, knights wore their armor proudly.

Armor was not only worn for battle but also for tournaments. Tournaments were festivals where the knights competed for fun. The **joust** was the main contest of the tournaments. During the joust, a knight would use a long spear or lance to try to knock another knight off his horse. The knights who won the joust would receive money, land, or other prizes.

Main Ideas

Answer the questions using the passage on page 18.

1. What is the main idea?
    A. Knights fought in battles.
    B. Knights were heroes a long time ago.
    C. Knights had a code of conduct.

2. Write *T* if the sentence is true. Write *F* if the sentence is false.

    _____ Knights used guns to fight battles.

    _____ Knights wore heavy suits called *armor* into battle.

    _____ A lance is a long spear.

    _____ The knight's armor weighed about 55 pounds (25 kg).

3. What is a *code of conduct*?
    A. a secret language knights used
    B. a set of rules knights had to follow
    C. a contest in a tournament

4. What is a *joust*?
    A. the knight's suit of armor, which was a symbol of honor, valor, and chivalry
    B. the prize for winning the battle
    C. a contest at a tournament where two knights battled with long spears

5. Circle the silent letter or letters in each word.

    A. knight   B. code   C. know

    D. rule   E. knock   F. compete

A *possessive pronoun* takes the place of a noun that shows belonging. Read each sentence.
Write the correct possessive pronoun in the blank.

6. Knights were loyal servants of _____their_____ king.

7. When jousting, a knight rode _____a_____ horse.

Helping at Home

Ask your child to name a time in history that he or she finds interesting. Go to the library with your child and pick out a book about this time period. Have your child share interesting things he or she is learning from the book each night at dinner.

Using Illustrations

Read the passage.

My Plate

The *My Plate* illustration shows the groups of foods you should eat every day to be healthy. The divided plate gives a picture of the different amounts of each type of food that should be eaten each day. Healthy foods, such as whole-grain breads, vegetables, fruits, and lean protein, should make up most of the food eaten every day. Smaller amounts of dairy should be eaten each day. Half your plate should be filled with fruits and vegetables. The other half of your plate should be filled with grains and protein.

The grain group is a major source of energy. This group contains foods such as bread, rice, and pasta. It is best to eat foods from this group that are marked "whole grain." The more active you are, the more servings you need from this group. The vegetable and fruit groups are next. Foods from the vegetable and fruit groups provide important **nutrients** to make the body healthy. The protein group is next. Lean proteins, such as beef, chicken, seafood, and beans, make up this group. This group also includes nuts and eggs. Foods from this group help make the body strong. Finally, consume a small amount of dairy products each day. Choices from this group should be fat-free or low-fat. Milk and low-fat foods from this group provide the calcium needed for strong bones and teeth.

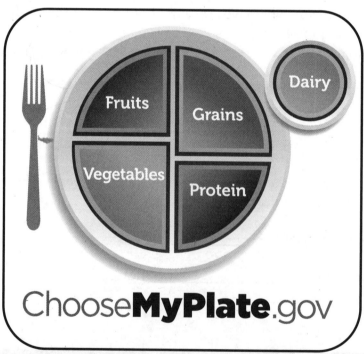

© U.S. Department of Agriculture or USDA

Using Illustrations

Answer the questions using the passage on page 20.

1. What is *My Plate*?
   A. a list of food the Egyptians ate
   B. a guide for healthy eating
   C. a shopping list

2. Write *T* if the sentence is true. Write *F* if the sentence is false.

   _____ Breads, cereals, rice, and pasta provide energy.

   _____ Don't ever eat any dairy.

   _____ Eat one serving from each group to be healthy.

   _____ Fruits and vegetables provide important nutrients for the body.

   _____ Milk and cheese provide calcium for strong bones and teeth.

3. What does the word *nutrients* mean?
   A. parts of foods that provide things our bodies need
   B. part of the nut family
   C. vitamins you get from eating certain fruits

4. Cross out the word that does not belong in each group.

A. apple	orange	milk	banana	pear
B. meat	candy bar	nuts	chicken	eggs
C. cheese	cereal	pasta	rice	bread

5. Write your five favorite foods. Which food group does each food belong to?

   _____

   _____

   _____

6. Look at the illustration.

   A. Which food group should you eat the most of? _____

   B. Which food group should you eat the least of? _____

Helping at Home

Plan a dinner menu with your child for the next week. Using the information on page 20, have your child draw what his or her dinner plate should look like each night. Let your child help you prepare the meals and portion the food on each plate.

Cause and Effect

Read the guidelines.

Bicycle Safety Guidelines
from Eisner Elementary School Safety Board

1. Always wear a helmet when you ride your bike. The helmet should have a snug fit and a strong strap and buckle.

2. Don't ride a bike that is too large for you. It may be hard to control. Make sure both feet can touch the ground when you are on the bike.

3. You should know how to stop the bike with the brakes. The brakes are usually on the handlebars. Some bikes use the pedals to brake.

4. Check your bike to make sure the tires, brakes, and other mechanical parts are in good working order.

5. Make sure you have permission to ride in the street. Ride on the right side of the road in single file.

6. Don't wear loose clothes. They may catch in the chain or wheels or on the pedals.

7. Observe traffic rules. Learn the correct hand signals for stopping and making turns.

8. Never ride with another person on your bike. It is hard enough to keep your balance without falling, much less with another person to balance as well.

9. Keep your hands and feet on the bike while riding.

10. Stay a safe distance behind other bike riders.

Cause and Effect

Answer the questions using the guidelines on page 22.

Can you match the parts of the bike to the picture? Write the number of the part in the blank.

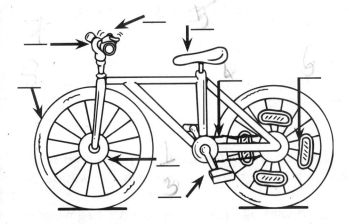

1. reflector
2. bell
3. pedal
4. chain
5. seat
6. spoke
7. handlebars
8. tire

Cause is why something happens. *Effect* is what takes place afterward. Read the rule number in parentheses. Predict what might happen if you don't follow the rule.

9. (Rule 3) _____

_____

10. (Rule 7) _____

_____

11. (Rule 9) _____

_____

Read each sentence. Circle the letter of the sentence in which the underlined word means the same as the word in the rule.

12. Rule 2
    A. Marla <u>ground</u> the meat for the hamburger patties.
    B. Make sure the apples don't fall to the <u>ground</u>.

13. Rule 4
    A. Afton wrote a <u>check</u> for her groceries.
    B. I will go and <u>check</u> to see if Simon is ready.

14. Rule 10
    A. Walking is a <u>safe</u> way to travel.
    B. The burglar broke into the <u>safe</u>.

15. Rule 5
    A. James thinks he is always <u>right</u>.
    B. Set the table with the knife on the <u>right</u> side of the plate.

16. Rule 7
    A. The queen <u>rules</u> the country of England.
    B. I hope the new principal doesn't give us too many <u>rules</u>.

17. Think of something people do that might be dangerous. Write it. Then, make a list of your own safety rules.

_____

A. _____

B. _____

C. _____

Helping at Home

Have your child write safety guidelines for something he or she likes to do, such as swimming or riding a scooter. Ask your child what would happen if a person did not follow those guidelines.

Sequencing and Visuals

Read the story.

Finding Poochy

Jared's grandmother can be quite forgetful. She is always losing things. Sometimes, she can't find her glasses when they are sitting on top of her head. Today, she lost her little dog, Poochy. She ran some errands this morning, and she took Poochy with her. Now, Poochy is missing. She asked Jared to help her find her dog.

"Tell me everything you can remember, Grandma," Jared said. Jared took notes as his grandmother recalled her morning.

"I walked out my front door and turned east," she remembered. "My first stop was to return some books at a place with a flag flying outside the building.

"Then, I went south and dropped off some cookies I had baked for Mrs. Green. She lives in a little house with a fence around the yard.

"Next, I walked west to the grocery store and picked up a few items. Luckily, I had a list so I remembered everything I needed. Poochy couldn't go into the store, so I tied him up outside by a tree.

"Then, I walked north one block. I stopped at a shop with a large bench outside. I remember the bench because I was pretty tired by this time. I sat on the bench to take a rest. I finished my errand at the shop and came home. I haven't seen Poochy since I stopped at that shop. It's a shame too, because I needed to take her for a shampoo and cut."

Sequencing and Visuals

Answer the questions using the story on page 24.

1. Where do you think Poochy is?

   Tied to the tree.

2. What clues will help Jared find Poochy?

   Probaly the clues that Jared's grandma gave him or her.

3. What does *recalled* mean in this story?

   (A.) did again

   B. remembered

   C. found

4. Number the sentences in the order that they happened.

   __3__ I stopped at a shop with a large bench outside.

   __2__ I tied Poochy outside by a tree.

   __1__ I dropped off some cookies at Mrs. Green's.

   __4__ I finished my errand at the shop.

Helping at Home

Have your child write a story that gives directions for finding something hidden in your neighborhood. Include a simple map. Then, take a walk together, following the directions given in the story. For added fun, have a treat waiting at the end.

Supporting Details

Read the passage.

Benjamin Franklin

Benjamin Franklin was born on January 17, 1705. He was a printer, a statesman, and an inventor.

At the age of 17, Franklin began working as a printer. He printed newspapers and books. He wrote many of the things he printed. In 1732, Franklin wrote and published *Poor Richard's Almanac*. He also printed all of the money for the state of Pennsylvania.

Franklin worked hard to make his state, Pennsylvania, a better place to live. He made improvements in the postal system and the police force. He established the first public library. He also helped start the first fire station after a fire destroyed much of the city of Philadelphia. He was elected a delegate from Pennsylvania to the Second Continental Congress in 1775. In 1776, he helped write the Declaration of Independence.

Franklin was also an inventor. He was always thinking of ways to do things faster and better. In 1741, he invented a stove that would heat up and remain at a certain temperature. He invented a type of glasses that he could use to help him read in his old age. He is probably best known for the important discoveries he made concerning electricity in 1752.

Benjamin Franklin died on April 17, 1790, at the age of 84. More than 20,000 people attended his funeral. He was an American hero who is still remembered today.

Supporting Details

Answer the following questions using the passage on page 26.

1. What is the main idea?
   A. Ben Franklin was an American hero.
   B. Ben Franklin should have been president of the United States.
   C. Ben Franklin was a great inventor.

2. Put an **X** by the things that are true about Benjamin Franklin.

   _____ He wrote books and newspaper articles.

   _____ He worked as a mail carrier.

   _____ He was the president of the United States.

   _____ He helped write the Declaration of Independence.

   _____ He discovered new facts about electricity.

3. Number the events in the order they occurred in Ben Franklin's life.

   _____ He died at the age of 84.

   _____ He became a delegate from Pennsylvania.

   _____ He worked as a printer.

   _____ He was born on January 17, 1705.

   _____ He made important discoveries about electricity.

4. An *obituary* is a notice about someone's death that usually includes details about the life they lived and major accomplishments. On another sheet of paper, write an obituary for Benjamin Franklin describing his life and his accomplishments.

The suffixes *–er* and *–or* mean "one who does." Add the correct suffix to each underlined word.

5. One who <u>invents</u> is called an
   inventor _____.

6. One who <u>prints</u> is called a
   printer _____.

7. One who <u>writes</u> is called a
   writer _____.

8. One who <u>helps</u> is called a
   helper _____.

Words like *after*, *although*, *because*, *until*, and *while* can be used to combine two sentences. Circle the word that can be used to combine two sentences into one. Write the new sentence.

9. Franklin invented a type of glasses. He wanted to be able to read in his old age.

   because   after

   Franklin invented a type of
   glasses because he wanted to

10. Franklin helped to start the first fire station. A fire destroyed much of Philadelphia.

   after   while

   Franklin helped to start the first
   fire station after a fire

11. Franklin is still an American hero today. He died on April 17, 1790.

   although   while

   Franklin is still an American hero
   today although he died on April 17, 1790.

Helping at Home

Have dinner with Benjamin Franklin! Help your child dress up as Benjamin Franklin and pretend to be him during dinnertime. Ask your child questions about Franklin's life and work and encourage your child to share details about his life.

Prefixes

A **prefix** is a group of letters at the beginning of a word that changes the word's meaning.

> **Example:** re + view = to look at again

Read the prefixes and their meanings. Use them to complete the activities below.

mid—middle	*post*—after	*non*—not	*uni*—one; single
re—again	*micro*—very small	*sub*—below	*pre*—before

Underline the base word in each word below. Then, write the meaning of the word.

1. midstream _the middle of a _____
2. preview _____
3. posttest _____
4. recharge _____
5. unicolor _____
6. microscope _tool used to _____ microscope _____
7. subzero _____
8. nonfiction _Not true _____

Write a word from the word bank to complete each sentence.

microchip	preheat	submarine
nonliving	reattach	unicycle

9. Rocks, cars, and books are all _____ things because they don't breathe or grow.

10. You have to have good balance to ride a _unicycle_.

11. Vets can place a _mic_ under a dog's skin because it is so small.

12. Many recipes ask you to _preheat_ the oven before doing anything else.

13. A _submarine_ can be hard to detect because it travels under the water.

14. Luke had to _reattach_ the pieces of his action figure after his little sister pulled it apart.

Helping
at Home

Name a prefix, such as *non-* or *re-*, and have your child list as many words using that prefix as he or she can think of in one minute. Then, play again with a different prefix. Keep playing until your child has listed a total of 30 or more words.

Suffixes

A **suffix** is a group of letters at the end of a word that changes the word's meaning. A suffix is added to the base word.

Example: acid + ify = acidify

Complete the chart. Use the suffix definitions to help you.

-able, -ible	able to be	-tion, -ation	changes a noun to a verb
-fy, -ify	to cause to become	-ment	the state of
-ty, -ity	changes a noun into an adjective		

Word	Suffix	Base Word	Use the word in a sentence.
celebration	-tion	celebrate	The celebration will honor her birthday.
1. education	tion	educa	Texas education children.
2. treatment	ment	treat	
3. glorify	fy	glory	
4. cruelty	ty	cruel	
5. collapsible	ible	collaps	
6. salutation	tion	saluta	you salutation.
7. washable	able	wash	It is washable.
8. notify	fy	notify	It is notify.

Have your child read through one chapter of his or her favorite book and, using a pencil, circle each word that contains a suffix. Go through the chapter together and have your child identify each base word.

Prefixes and Suffixes

A **prefix** is a group of letters that is added to the beginning of a base word to change the word's meaning.

A **suffix** is a group of letters that is added to the end of a base word to change the word's meaning.

Read the prefixes and suffixes and their meanings.

over—too much	*trans*—across	*-er*—one who	*-ful*—full of
pre—before	*mis*—wrongly	*-est*—most	*-less*—without

Underline the base word in each word. Then, write the meaning of the word.

1. transplant _____

2. helpful _____

3. worker _____

4. overgrown _____

5. misunderstand _____

6. hopeless _____

Write a word from the word bank to complete each sentence.

misspell	painless	thankful
overspend	teacher	transport

7. We are _____thankful_____ that we have an extra day to study for the test.

8. Mark said that the bee sting was _____painless_____, but it looked like it hurt.

9. My mom told us not to _____overspend_____ at the store.

10. I was very excited when the _____teacher_____ explained our field trip.

11. The boats _____transport_____ goods from one dock to another.

12. The teacher asks us to be careful and not _____misspell_____ words when we are writing.

Helping at Home Write a variety of prefixes, base words, and suffixes on index cards and place them in a bag. Take turns drawing one card at a time with your child. Whoever can create the most words that use either a prefix or a suffix before the bag is empty, wins!

Open Syllables

All words are made of at least one **syllable**. A syllable has one vowel sound and one consonant or more. The consonants change the sound the vowel makes or may have their sounds changed by the vowel.

A syllable that ends with a vowel and makes a long vowel sound is an **open syllable**.

Write how many syllables are in each word. Then, underline each open syllable.

bacon _2_   bagels _2_   begins _2_   cocoa _____

cider _2_   delicious _3_   excited _3_   final _____

flavors _____   lilacs _2_   music _____   navy _____

photographs _2_ remember _____   resist _2_   silent _____

table _____   tidy _2_

Use words from above to complete the paragraph. The number after the blank tells the number of syllables in that word.

Lucy is planning a breakfast party. She will fry _____bacon_____(2) and sausage. Some of her friends like bread and others like _____bagels_____(2). She bought jelly and two different

_____flavors_____(2) of cream cheese. Lucy will serve apple _____cider_____(2) and hot

_____cocoa_____(2). Lucy is _____excited_____(3) to decorate the _____table_____(2).

She bought a _____lilacs_____(2)-and-white striped tablecloth. Then, she filled baskets

with _____lilacs_____(2) and ivy. The _____final_____(2) thing she does is choose

peaceful _____music_____(2). She doesn't want a _____silent_____(2) party. Lucy can't

_____resist_____(2) piano tunes, so she downloads several songs. When Lucy's guests arrive,

she _____begins_____(2) to serve the food. She takes _____photographs_____(3) so she will

_____remember_____(3) the event. As her guests finish eating, they help her

_____tidy_____(2) up the kitchen. Everyone thanks Lucy for a _____navy_____(3)

breakfast party.

Closed Syllables

A syllable that ends with a consonant and has a short vowel sound is a **closed syllable**.

Count how many syllables are in the words below. Then, underline each closed syllable.

after __2__   animals __3__   broccoli __3__   carrots __2__

circles __2__   computers _____   electricity __5__   enjoy _____

follow __2__   galaxy _____   habit _____   hamster __2__

lettuce __2__   library _____   pencils _____   pictures __2__

planetarium __5__   planets _____   playful __2__   system _____

topics __2__

Use words from above to complete the paragraph. The number after the blank tells the number of syllables in that word.

Our class studies many interesting _____(2). My favorite unit

was about _____(2). I drew _____(2) of the solar

_____(2). Next week, we are going to the _____(5). I'm very

excited! We will learn about constellations and our _____(3).

I also love learning about _____(3). We have a class _____

(2). We take turns feeding him fresh vegetables like _____(3) and

_____(2). Sometimes, he eats _____(2), too. Our hamster is

very _____(2)! He likes to _____(2) his tail around and run in

_____(2). He also has a _____(2) of scratching his nose.

_____(2) school, my friends and I help our teacher. I sharpen the

_____(2). My friends tidy up our classroom _____(3). We turn

off all of the _____(3) and the lights to save _____(5). We

_____(2) helping our teacher.

© Carson-Dellosa • CD-704503

Helping at Home

Give your child a clapping rhythm such as 3 claps/3 claps/2 claps. Then, have your child think of words whose syllables match the number of claps, such as com-pu-ters, an-i-mals, af-ter. Have your child clap the rhythm while saying the words.

Context Clues

At times, you may not recognize a word or know its meaning, but **context clues** in a sentence can help you to figure it out.

One context clue can be a word's part of speech.

> **Example:** The carpet's colors <u>harmonize</u> with those of the walls and furniture. (Decide what part of speech the underlined word is, what function it has in the sentence, and what it actually means.)

Another context clue can be the other words in the sentence.

> **Example:** The team was <u>forlorn</u> after losing the game. (The other words tell you that the team was sad.)

Use context clues to complete each sentence with one of the words in parentheses.

1. _____Astronomy_____ is one of Tom's favorite subjects. (Astronaut, Astronomy, Atmosphere)

2. He ____especially____ liked to follow the movement of the stars. (especially, establish, exceptionally)

3. Tom was delighted when his family gave him a _____Uroscope_____ for his birthday. (telegram, telephoned, telescope)

4. Part of his birthday present was to go camping with his father in a park where _____conditions_____ were good for stargazing. (constellations, conditions, conjunctions)

5. When the night came for Tom to go to the park, he took the necessary equipment with which to make his _____observation_____. (observes, orbits, observations)

6. Tom saw several _____constellation_____, including Orion and the dippers. (consultants, constellations, confirmations)

7. He drew pictures of what he saw and recorded their positions using a _____compass_____. (compass, confess, congress)

Helping at Home

Have your child read aloud a story from a newspaper or magazine. When your child comes to an unfamiliar word, help him or her look for context clues to guess its meaning. Then, look up the word in the dictionary to confirm the definition.

Context Clues

Read the passage.

The rocky land of the northern forests in North America was never good for farming. Without fish and game, the early **natives** would have starved. Their lives were **dependent** on the animals they hunted.

In order to survive, the early Native Americans of the North American forests played games. The games used the skills they needed to be successful in their hunting. They needed to be able to judge distances, pick up clues and signs from their environment, and **conceal** themselves from the animals they hunted. In one of the games the Native Americans played, the men threw axes. In another, they took turns throwing spears or sticks into a hoop on the ground. Such games improved the players' **accuracy**.

Moose and caribou were very important to the tribes. Moose usually lived and traveled by themselves. Caribou **migrated** in herds across a large area each season. The Native Americans **stalked** the moose from one **range** to another. When hunting caribou, they would wait for them at a place along the caribou's trails.

Weirs, nets, traps, hooks, and spears were used to catch fish. Whitefish and jackfish were caught in lakes, and Arctic grayling and trout were caught in rivers. The Native Americans fished from the shore or in canoes in summer and through holes cut in the ice in winter.

After the ice melted, the traps were set. Sometimes, when meat was **scarce**, the Native Americans would eat rabbit, mink, or wolverine. When hunting became poor, they lived on dried meat and fish. They also ate pemmican, a mixture of dried meat and animal fat.

Write each bold word from the passage next to its definition.

1. open area on which animals roam _range_

2. not plentiful, skimpy _scarce_

3. original inhabitants _natives_

4. relying on something else _dependent_

5. chased prey _stalked_

6. quality of being exact _accuracy_

7. hide _conceal_

8. went from one place to another _migrated_

Helping at Home
Have your child make up a silly word, such as *grwarble*, and write a sentence that uses the word and includes context clues to its meaning. Read the sentence and guess the meaning of the word. Take turns writing silly words and sentences.

Context Clues

Read the passage.

The Space Age began in 1957 when the former Union of Soviet Socialist Republics (USSR) **launched** the first satellite. It was named *Sputnik 1*. The importance of its mission **transformed** how the world was able to look at space. *Sputnik 1* was the first object to go beyond Earth's **atmosphere**. Since then, thousands of satellites have been launched, mostly by the **former** USSR and the United States. Today, the satellites are much larger and heavier. Some weigh several tons, and their **payloads** have a purpose related to each satellite's **mission**. Today's satellites are designed to perform different tasks, such as exploring Earth and space, observing the weather, improving communications, and assisting the military.

Until the Space Age, many **theories** about space could not be proven. They could only be **evaluated** from observations and with instruments on the ground. The gases within the atmosphere that surrounds Earth **distort** the way the stars really look. Putting satellites beyond Earth's atmosphere can help scientists get a better picture of distant stars and maybe the **universe**.

Write each bold word in the passage next to its definition.

1. the layers of gases surrounding a planet _____atmosphere_____

2. initiated, released _____launced_____

3. determined, tested _____evaluted_____

4. a specific task _____mission_____

5. changed _____transformed_____

6. twist the normal shape _____distort_____

7. before in time _____theories_____

8. beliefs, analyses of a set of facts _____former_____

9. everything in space _____universe_____

10. loads carried by a satellite necessary for the flight _____payloads_____

Writing to Persuade

When **writing to persuade**, the author wants the reader to agree with his or her opinion. Before writing, answer the questions:

- *What* is your opinion?
- *Whom* are you trying to convince?
- *Why* do you think that others should agree with your opinion?

Imagine that your teacher has decided to break the class into small groups for a project. Should students be allowed to choose whom they want to work with? Use the graphic organizer to help you plan your persuasive paragraph.

What is your opinion on the topic?

_es,_

Whom are you trying to persuade?

The teacher

Why do you think that others should agree with your opinion? List three reasons to support your opinion.

1. _I ___ will __ fun._

2. _The teacher ___ to break __ to __ groups._

3. _I ___ be easier __ work with._

On another sheet of paper, use your notes to help you write a five-sentence persuasive paragraph.

Helping at Home

Ask your child what someone taking the opposite opinion about the topic on this page might say. Have your child list reasons to support the opposite point of view. Does your child still stand by his or her original opinion?

Writing to Inform

When **writing to inform**, authors can use personal ideas and feelings to explain different topics.

Everyone has a favorite place. Explain why your favorite place is special to you. Complete the chart to express your ideas and feelings on the topic.

Topic My Favorite Place Is ___Disney Land___

Reason #1 I like this place because
___there is a lot of fun rides.___

Reason #2 I like this place because
___it is big___

Example
___Like the water slides.___

Example
___there is a big parks___

Details
___slides have water in
_____ your water
so it the end you are
wet.___

Details
___the tm ... ferris
there ... kind of
.... and
and and many ... more.___

Helping at Home

Have your child write several paragraphs about his or her favorite place using the reasons, examples, and details from this page. Encourage your child to draw a picture of the place, too. Display your child's completed writing and artwork.

Compare and Contrast

When authors **compare and contrast** two objects or ideas, they tell how they are alike and how they are different.

Think about two objects, events, or places to compare and contrast. Fill in the chart with the details. Then, use the flowchart to help you write two paragraphs on another sheet of paper. In the paragraphs, compare and contrast the topic.

Topic _____ and _____

How They Are Alike
(Key Words: *both, common, like, same*)

How They Are Different
(Key Words: *but, different, however, unlike*)

Example

1. _____
   _____
2. _____
   _____
3. _____
   _____
4. _____
   _____

Example

1. _____
   _____
2. _____
   _____
3. _____
   _____
4. _____
   _____

Example

1. _____
   _____
2. _____
   _____
3. _____
   _____
4. _____
   _____

Helping at Home

Ask your child to draw a Venn diagram and use it to compare himself or herself to a friend. Suggest specific examples about how the two are alike and different. Then, have your child write two paragraphs based on details from the diagram.

Parts of a Story

A story should have a beginning, a middle, and an end. These parts help the reader follow the story without getting confused. The **beginning** of a story usually introduces the characters. The **middle** is where the plot of the story unfolds, and a problem may be presented. The **end** completes the story and may solve the problem.

In this story, a girl named Lucy is afraid of monsters. The middle of the story has been written for you. Write a beginning and an end to complete the story.

Beginning

O_____ _____ young _____ _____ _____
_____ _____ "I _____ find out
what _____ _____ she exclaimed.

Middle

   "Tonight," Lucy proclaimed, "I will face my fears!" As Lucy was getting ready for bed, she took the flashlight out of her dresser drawer. Lucy carefully tucked the flashlight under her pillow and climbed into bed. She waited a few minutes before she whispered, "OK, it's now or never. I must find out if creatures really are hiding under my bed." Lucy took a deep breath, grabbed the flashlight, and braced herself. She sprang out of bed and shouted, "Here I come!" Lucy flashed the bright beam of light under the bed. "Just as I suspected," she laughed.

End

A_____ _____ _____ _____ her _____ _____
_____ _____ the _____ _____
_____ her _____
_____ _____ _____ _____ beds!

Helping at Home

Build stories with your child while on the go. Start a story at the beginning, middle, or end, and take turns with your child filling in the gaps of the story. Discuss things that make a good beginning or ending for a story.

Plot

The **plot** is what happens in a story. A strong plot includes not only the problem and a solution but also a series of events that leads to the ending.

Many children believe that they should have later bedtimes. Complete a writing plan for a story about a girl who tries to get her parents to let her stay up an hour past her bedtime. Fill in the missing details on the flowchart. Use the flowchart to help you write the story on another sheet of paper.

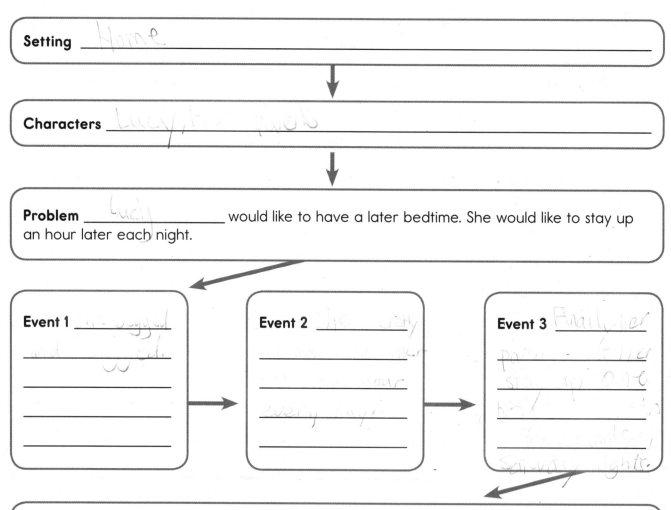

Setting _Home_

Characters _Lucy, the parents_

Problem _Lucy_ would like to have a later bedtime. She would like to stay up an hour later each night.

Event 1 _she begged and asked_

Event 2 _she ... ask ... our every day_

Event 3 _Finally her parents... her stay up one hour ... Saturday nights._

Solution: Her parents allow her to stay up an extra hour on Friday and Saturday nights only.

Helping at Home

Watch your child's favorite movie together. Have your child outline the plot of the movie, identifying the settings, characters, central problem, and solution. Discuss ways the plot would be different without the problem.

Strong Story Beginnings

Good authors grab the reader's attention from the start. A strong **beginning** will make the reader want to continue reading.

Think about a time when you or someone you know found something unexpected. Write a terrific beginning for your story using action or dialogue. Use words from the word bank to help.

Action and Dialogue Word Bank

amazed	discovered	gasped
confused	exclaimed	investigated
demanded	explored	replied

_____

_____

_____

_____

_____

_____

_____

_____

_____

_____

Annibel

Helping at Home

Think of a recent exciting event you experienced. Write the beginning of a story about the event, making sure to include few descriptive details. Have your child rewrite what you wrote, using action and dialogue to grab the reader's attention.

Time-Order Words

Time-order words help authors organize their thoughts. These words can connect one sentence to the next. Time-order words help the reader understand the order of events.

Examples: *eventually, finally, first, last, next, now, shortly, after, soon, then*

Read the paragraph. The time-order words have been left out. On each line, write a time-order word to complete the sentence.

Monday mornings are always hectic for me. Mom and Dad have a lot for me to do before I can leave for school. ___First___, I have to take a warm shower. This always helps me wake up and get ready for the day ahead. ___Next___, I put on my clothes. This part is easy because I wear my school uniform each day. ___Then___, I have to make my bed. I can't even think about having breakfast until I make my bed. ___Now___, I have to wake my little brother. He gets to sleep later than I do. I try to wake him slowly. ___First___, I whisper his name. ___Next___, I give him a gentle push. If that doesn't work, I have no choice but to yell, "Tommy, get up!" That usually does the trick. ___Eventually___, my stomach starts growling. So, I eat a bowl of cereal. On Monday mornings, we have no time for fluffy pancakes. I ___then___ brush my teeth and comb my hair. I can ___finally___ head off to school!

Helping at Home

Write time-order words from this page on index cards and flip them over. Then, have your child start telling a story. Every sentence or so, have your child flip over an index card and use the word before continuing the story.

Writing Story Endings

Good authors use satisfying **endings** to make what they are writing feel complete. A satisfying ending can be either positive or negative, but it should create a strong finish.

Read the story details. Write one ending by summarizing the main idea and another ending by hinting at what is to come.

Character

Barbara is nine years old. Her parents give her a weekly allowance of five dollars for doing her chores.

Problem

Barbara wants to buy a new video game system.

Solution

She saves her weekly allowance to purchase the video game system. After six months, she has saved enough money to buy it.

Satisfying Ending: Summarizing the Main Idea

_____

_____

_____

_____

Satisfying Ending: Hinting at What Is to Come

_____

_____

_____

_____

Helping at Home

Ask your child to think of a book or movie that has a disappointing ending. Discuss what could make the ending better. Then, encourage your child to write a new ending for the story and read it to you.

Writing Story Endings

Read the story details. Write a satisfying ending to the story by either summarizing the main idea or hinting at what is to come.

Character
Ansley is 10 years old. He is hardworking but not athletic.

Problem
Ansley wants to learn how to play soccer. He has always wanted to be on a team.

Solution
He practices with his dad every day until he tries out for the school soccer team. He makes the team.

Satisfying Ending

_____

_____

_____

_____

_____

_____

_____

_____

_____

_____

_____

 Helping at Home

Ask your child to think of something he or she had to work hard to achieve. Have your child write a story about the experience, paying special attention to making the conclusion strong.

Writing with Purpose

Focused writing targets one specific, small topic. It tells a lot about one thing or moment. All of the details are important to the main idea. Focused writing does not have any extra or unimportant information. It stays on topic.

Unfocused writing is about too many things. It tells a little bit about various topics. Some details are not important or have nothing to do with the main idea. This can make it hard for the reader to follow the story.

Think about a time when you went to an exciting place. List several exciting parts of your trip.

_____

_____

_____

_____

_____

Write a focused story about your trip. To help focus your writing, think about a specific moment on your trip that was especially great. Use another sheet of paper if needed.

_____

_____

_____

_____

_____

_____

_____

Helping at Home Have your child keep a journal for a week where he or she practices focused writing. At the end of each day, ask your child to think of one particular moment from the day that was especially memorable and write a paragraph about it.

Writing with Purpose

When authors write, they think about why they are writing. They also keep their **audience** in mind. Writing with purpose helps authors communicate their ideas to the correct audience.

Think about a story. Answer the questions.

1. Who will read your story? _____

_____

2. Why do you want people to read your story? _____

_____

_____

3. Write an introductory sentence that will be interesting for your readers. _____

_____

_____

4. Make a list of words that will make your story interesting or exciting for your readers.

_____

_____

_____

5. Write a rough draft.

6. Read your draft. Complete the checklist.

❏   Is it interesting or exciting?

❏   Does your story have a clear focus?

❏   Did you use proper capitalization and punctuation?

❏   Do you need to correct any misspelled words?

❏   Did you use proper grammar?

Helping at Home

Have your child write a paragraph about his or her favorite sport for a friend. Then, have your child write a paragraph on the same topic for his or her teacher. Ask your child how the paragraphs are different.

Revising and Editing

Good authors plan before they write. Then, when they finish writing, they carefully **revise and edit** what they have written.

Use the outline below to help you plan, revise, and edit a piece of writing.

Planning

- What is your topic? _____

- List three details about your topic.

  _____

  _____

  _____

Writing

- Write your story or essay on a separate sheet of paper. When you are done, use your writing to complete the steps below.

Revising

- Is the introduction clear? _____ Why or why not? _____

  _____

- Does the piece make sense? _____ Why or why not? _____

  _____

- Does each paragraph have a topic sentence? _____ What is it? _____

  _____

- Does the conclusion restate the introduction? _____ How? _____

  _____

Editing

- ❏ Fix the misspelled words.
- ❏ Correct the grammatical errors.
- ❏ Correct the punctuation errors.
- ❏ Change the run-on sentences and fragments.

Helping at Home

Have your child review something he or she wrote recently. Ask your child to follow the steps on this page to identify ways to improve the writing. Then, have your child rewrite the piece and display it somewhere the whole family can see.

Research Project

When writing a **research project**, an author starts by choosing a topic. Then, the author researches the topic and presents the information in an interesting or fun format.

1. Choose an animal to write about. _____

2. Use books or the Internet to research each of the three categories below. Write the information you find.

The Animal's Appearance

_____

_____

_____

The Animal's Habitat

_____

_____

_____

The Animal's Diet

_____

_____

_____

3. Use the information you find to write five paragraphs. Write an interesting introductory paragraph. Then, write one paragraph about each category above. Finally, write a concluding paragraph.

4. Draw an illustration to go along with your project.

Helping at Home

Have your child use computer software to create a magazine about animals in which his or her completed research project will appear. The magazine could include a cover, illustrations, and more articles about animals.

Linking Verbs

A **linking verb** does not show action. It links the subject of a sentence to a noun, pronoun, or adjective in the predicate. Present tense forms of the verb **be**—*am*, *is*, and *are*—and forms of the verb **have**—*have* and *had*—are common linking verbs. **Appear**, **become**, **feel**, **look**, **seem**, **smell**, **taste**, and **turn** can also be used as linking verbs.

Example: The day <u>is</u> August 24, 79 A.D. (<u>Is</u> links the noun in the subject to the noun in the predicate.)

Write *action* if a verb is an action verb or *linking* if a verb is a linking verb.

1. seems _____

2. explore _____

3. crashes _____

4. escape _____

5. feels _____

6. floats _____

7. shake _____

8. trace _____

9. surrenders _____

10. become _____

Write the correct present tense form of each verb in parentheses.

11. The day _____ as any other day in Pompeii. (begins, begin)

12. Children play, and shopkeepers _____ their goods. (sell, sells)

13. People _____ at the Forum to discuss current events. (gather, gathers)

14. Suddenly, at midday, Mount Vesuvius _____. (explode, explodes)

15. The 20,000 people in Pompeii _____ in every direction. (dashes, dash)

16. Hot ash and pumice _____ down on the city. (rain, rains)

17. Some people _____ this disaster by boat. (escapes, escape)

18. Two feet of ash _____ Pompeii within hours of the eruption. (covers, cover)

Compare two passages from a book, newspaper, or magazine. Have your child count how many linking verbs and action verbs he or she sees in each passage. Which type of verb seems to be used more frequently?

Adjectives

An **adjective** is a word that describes a noun. It can tell how many or what kind. An adjective often appears in front of the noun it describes.

> **Example:** Lou raises <u>woolly</u> llamas on his ranch. (<u>Woolly</u> describes the <u>llamas</u>.)

An adjective can appear after a linking verb. A linking verb can link the subject of a sentence with an adjective in the predicate.

> **Example:** Llamas are <u>lovable</u>. (<u>Are</u> links the noun <u>llamas</u> in the subject with the adjective <u>lovable</u> in the predicate.)

A noun may have more than one adjective.

> **Example:** Lou raises <u>lovable</u>, <u>woolly</u> llamas on his ranch.

Write the adjective or adjectives that describe each underlined noun.

1. <u>Llamas</u> are usually gentle and friendly. ___Gentle, Friendly___

2. They have big, beautiful <u>eyes</u>. ___Big, Beautiful___

3. Llamas have split upper <u>lips</u> like camels. ___Split___

4. They have thick wool <u>coats</u>. ___Thick___

5. Their hair can be made into soft <u>sweaters</u> and blankets. ___Soft___

6. <u>Llamas</u> are smart and can be trained easily. ___Smart___

7. Lou can lead a llama on a long <u>leash</u>. ___Long___

8. <u>Llamas</u> are sure-footed on trails. ___Sure-footed___

9. They are wonderful pack <u>animals</u>. ___Wonderful Pack___

10. Llamas have two-toed <u>feet</u> that do not damage trails. ___Two-twoed___

Helping at Home

Ask your child to write a paragraph about the weather outside using no adjectives. Then, have your child rewrite the paragraph using many descriptive adjectives. Read the two paragraphs out loud. Which one sounds more interesting?

Adverbs

An **adverb** describes how, when, or where the action of a verb takes place. Adverbs that tell how usually end with *ly*.

Draw a circle around each adverb. Underline the verb it modifies. Write *how*, *when*, or *where* to tell how the adverb modifies the verb.

how 1. The knight (bravely) <u>fought</u> the dragon.

how 2. The clown foolishly chased the little dog.

how 3. Mike walked downstairs.

where 4. The class played today.

where 5. I lost my ring somewhere.

where 6. The boat sailed away.

how 7. She played the game honestly.

how 8. The teacher carefully fed the fish.

where 9. My sister is coming tomorrow.

where 10. Mom planted the flowers outside.

Complete each sentence with an adverb that tells how, when, or where.

11. Lisa took the dog _____by_____. (how)

12. Lisa took the dog _____in the morning_____. (when)

13. Lisa took the dog _____to the park_____. (where)

14. Danny _____carefully_____ watched the dog. (how)

Comparative Adverbs

An **adverb** is a word that describes how, when, or where the action of a verb takes place. Add **-er** to one-syllable adverbs to compare two actions. Add **-est** to one-syllable adverbs to compare more than two actions.

Examples: hard/hard<u>er</u>/hard<u>est</u>

Adverbs often end with **-ly**. Use **more** before these adverbs to compare two actions. Use **most** before these adverbs to compare more than two actions.

Examples: quickly/<u>more</u> quickly/<u>most</u> quickly

Write the forms of each adverb that can compare the actions of verbs.

Adverbs	Adverbs That Compare Two Actions	Adverbs That Compare More Than Two Actions
1. loud	louder	loudest
2. slow	slower	slowest
3. fast	faster	fastest
4. closely	closer	closest
5. calmly		
6. quietly		quietest
7. smoothly	mother	smoothest
8. softly	fter	softtes

Write the correct adverb.

9. The windows _____ shook. (suddenly, more suddenly)

10. Caleb can run _____ than the entire class. (fast, faster)

11. The salesperson shook our hands _____. (warmly, most warmly)

Challenge your child to run a certain distance three different times in one day. Have your child write down the amount of time it takes him or her to run. Then, have your child write several sentences comparing the three times using comparative adverbs.

Object Pronouns

An **object pronoun** is used in the predicate of a sentence. It receives the action of the verb. *Him, her, it, us,* and *them* are object pronouns that can replace nouns.

> **Example:** Thunderstorms frighten my brother.
> Thunderstorms frighten <u>him</u>.

You and *me* are object pronouns that can stand alone.

> **Example:** The manager of the grocery store told <u>you</u> and <u>me</u> about the jobs.

Write *him, her, it, us,* or *them* to replace each word or group of words.

1. Carlos _____ him _____

2. clouds _____ it _____

3. Carmen _____ her _____

4. water _____ it _____

5. rain _____ it _____

6. Carlos and me _____ us _____

7. lightning _____ it _____

8. sound waves _____ (they) _____

Write *him, her, it, us,* or *them* to replace the bold word or group of words in each sentence.

9. Mother calls **Carlos and me** to come inside the house. _____ (us) _____

10. She knows that big, black clouds signal **a thunderstorm**. _____ it _____

11. We see flashes of lightning in **the clouds**. _____ it _____

12. The lightning frightens **Carmen**. _____ him _____

13. We hear the rain begin to fall on **the roof**. _____ it _____

14. Strong winds blow **the trees**. _____ them _____

15. We listen to **the rumbling and booming of the thunder**. _____ them _____

Helping at Home

Have your child tell a story about something that happened at school that involves one or more friends. Challenge your child to use only object pronouns while telling the story. For extra fun, see if you can guess who the pronouns stand for!

Nouns ✓

A **singular noun** names one person, place, or thing.

> **Example:** The <u>boy</u> plays softball.

A **plural noun** names more than one person, place, or thing. It often ends in s or es.

> **Example:** The <u>boys</u> play on a team.

A **collective noun** names a group of people or things. It is considered a singular noun in a sentence if the word is used as a unit.

> **Example:** The <u>team</u> was in first place. (<u>Was</u> is a singular verb.)

Write *S* if a noun is singular, *P* if it is plural, or *C* if it is collective.

_____ 1. audience   _____ 2. crowd   _____ 3. government

_____ 4. biscuits   _____ 5. icicle   _____ 6. valley

_____ 7. errand   _____ 8. committee   _____ 9. flock

_____ 10. crew   _____ 11. sandwiches   _____ 12. stack

_____ 13. hydrants   _____ 14. morsel   _____ 15. family

Write the collective noun from the word bank that names each group of animals. Refer to a dictionary if needed.

gaggle	litter	plague	school
herd	pack	pod	swarm

16. _____ of puppies   17. _____ of bees

18. _____ of geese   19. _____ of locusts

20. _____ of whales   21. _____ of fish

22. _____ of elephants   23. _____ of wolves

24. Use each collective noun in a sentence. Write them on another sheet of paper.

Helping at Home Together with your child, write singular, plural, and collective nouns on self-stick notes and stick them to a wall. Create a silly story, one sentence at a time. Take turns randomly selecting a noun and using it in a sentence that adds to the story.

Nouns

A **concrete noun** is a word that names a person, place, or thing. A concrete noun identifies someone or something that can be seen, heard, smelled, touched, or tasted.

Examples: <u>actor</u> (person), <u>theater</u> (place), <u>play</u> (thing)

An **abstract noun** is a word that names an idea or quality that has no physical existence.

Examples: <u>suggestion</u>, <u>kindness</u>

Write each concrete noun from the word bank under the correct heading.

awning	cabinet	infant	mansion	pharmacy	studio
bachelor	fortress	lobby	orphan	satellite	table
bride	hexagon	maiden	partner	souvenir	university

Person	Place	Thing
bride	studio	Cabinet
Infant	fortress	souvenir
Partner	pharmacy	satelite
Maiden	Lobby	Hexagon
bachelor	Mansion	Table
Orphan	University	Awning

Write **concrete** or **abstract** to identify each of the nouns below.

1. revenge _Abstract_

2. bravery _Abtract_

3. textile _____

4. imagination _Abstract_

5. orchestra _Concrete_

6. freedom _Abstract_

7. On another sheet of paper, write a sentence using each abstract noun you identified in questions 1 to 6.

Look through old photos with your child. Ask your child to use both concrete nouns and abstract nouns to describe the pictures. For example, a picture could show two girls (concrete) or friendship (abstract).

Verbs

A **past tense action verb** shows action that has already happened. The past tense of most action verbs is made by adding **ed** to the present tense verb.

Example: talk/talk<u>ed</u>

However, if the verb ends in a silent **e**, just add **d**.

Example: smile/smil<u>ed</u>

If the verb ends with a single consonant preceded by a single vowel, double the consonant and add **ed**.

Example: flap/flap<u>ped</u>

If the verb ends in a consonant followed by **y**, change the **y** to **i** and add **ed**.

Example: study/stud<u>ied</u>

Write the past tense form of each present tense action verb.

1. delay _____

2. help _____

3. place _____

4. arrive _____

5. slip _____

6. trim _____

7. magnify _____

8. propel _____

Write the past tense form of each present tense verb in parentheses.

9. In 1860, Hank _____ for a job in the newspaper. (look)

10. The 16-year-old boy _____ to be a Pony Express rider. (want)

11. He _____ and was accepted for the extremely dangerous job. (apply)

12. As a Pony Express rider, Hank _____ the US mail between swing stations that were 50 to 100 miles apart. (carry)

13. Relay stations between swing stations _____ him with fresh horses. (supply)

Helping at Home

Have your child write a paragraph about his or her day using present tense verbs such as *talk* and *play*. Tomorrow, have your child rewrite the paragraph using past tense verbs such as *talked* and *played*.

Irregular Verbs

Most **past tense verbs** are formed by adding **ed** to the present tense forms. **Irregular past tense verbs** are formed differently.

Examples:	**Present Tense**	**Past Tense**
	I <u>see</u> it today.	I <u>saw</u> it yesterday.

Write the past tense form of each irregular verb. Look up the present tense verb in a dictionary to learn the past tense if needed.

Present Tense	Past Tense		Present Tense	Past Tense
1. shoot	shot		2. teach	taught
3. draw	drew		4. find	found
5. speak	spoke		6. feel	felt
7. hold	held		8. write	wrote
9. hear	heard		10. catch	caught

Rewrite each sentence using the past tense form of each underlined irregular verb.

11. I <u>see</u> a monarch butterfly on a milkweed plant.

_____ monarch butterfly on a milkweed plant.

12. The butterfly <u>makes</u> its egg sticky.

The butterfly made its egg sticky.

13. The tiny white egg <u>sticks</u> to the leaf.

The tiny white egg sticked to the leaf.

14. A small caterpillar <u>comes</u> out of the egg.

A small caterpillar came out of the egg.

Helping at Home

Write each irregular past tense verb from this page on a colorful strip of paper. Glue the strips of paper together to make a paper chain. Have your child add a new irregular past tense verb to the paper chain every day for one month.

Comparative Adjectives ✓

An **adjective** can be used to compare people, places, or things. Add **-er** to most adjectives to compare two nouns. Add **-est** to compare more than two nouns.

> **Examples:** bright/bright<u>er</u>/bright<u>est</u>

If an adjective ends with **e**, just add **r** to compare two nouns. Just add **st** to compare more than two nouns.

> **Examples:** white/whit<u>er</u>/whit<u>est</u>

If an adjective ends in a consonant that comes after a short vowel sound, double the final consonant and add **-er** or **-est**.

> **Examples:** thin/thin<u>ner</u>/thin<u>nest</u>

Write the forms of each adjective that can compare nouns.

Adjective	Adjectives That Compare Two Nouns	Adjectives That Compare More Than Two Nouns
1. long		
2. broad	broader	broadest
3. large		larger
4. flat		flattest
5. sweet		
6. wide	wider	widest
7. cool	cooler	coolest
8. smart	smarter	smartest

© Carson-Dellosa • CD-704503

Helping at Home — Ask your child to find several interesting objects such as toys, articles of clothing, or things from nature. Have your child compare them using comparative adjectives. Compare two objects to each other, then add a third object to compare.

Conjunctions

A **conjunction** is used to connect words, phrases, clauses, and sentences. Some common conjunctions are **and**, **but**, and **or**. They are also called **coordinating conjunctions**.

And connects two similar things or ideas.

> **Example:** I like spinach, <u>and</u> James likes squash.

But connects two different ideas.

> **Example:** January is in the winter, <u>but</u> July is in the summer.

Or connects two choices.

> **Example:** We may go to the beach, <u>or</u> we may go to the lake.

Write *and*, *but*, or *or* in each sentence.

1. Jenna _____and_____ Ryan are on the same baseball team.

2. She wanted the team color to be blue, _____but_____ he preferred red.

3. Everyone chose their favorite positions, _____and_____ they were very pleased.

4. Jenna either plays first base, _____ she plays in the outfield.

5. In the first inning, Jenna hit a single _____and_____ Ryan hit a double.

6. Their team was winning, _____ the other team caught up in the fourth inning.

7. Jenna stopped one runner, _____ Ryan let the other runner get to third base.

8. The other team had three runs, _____but_____ the score was tied.

9. Ryan hit a home run, _____a_____ his team earned two more runs.

10. To celebrate their win, Jenna and Ryan may go out for pizza, _____or_____ they may go out for ice cream.

Helping at Home

Give your child two silly phrases such as *I train dancing hippos* and *I fight ninja kangaroos*. Then, have your child combine them in sentences using different conjunctions. Discuss how the conjunctions change the meanings of the sentences.

Quotation Marks

do again!

> **Quotation marks** are used around the exact words that someone speaks.
>
> **Examples:** "How was your day today?" Mom asked.
> "It was great," Tiffany replied. "I had a lot of fun."

Rewrite the sentences. Add commas, quotation marks, and capital letters where needed.

1. are you ready to leave? Grandpa asked. _"Are you ready to leave?" Grandpa asked._

2. I had a huge breakfast this morning Miguel said. _I had a huge breakfast this morning," Miguel said._

3. Libby said wait for me! I don't want to be late. _Libby said, "Wait for me! I don't want to be late._

4. I stubbed my toe on the way to the bus stop Jack moaned. _"I stubbed my toe on the way to the bus stop," Jack moaned._

5. hooray! I won the race! Riley exclaimed. _"hooray! I won the race!" Riley exclaimed._

6. Would you like a slice of apple pie? Mrs. Havel asked. _"Would you like a slice of apple pie?" Mrs. Havel asked._

7. Ryan said I would like to go for a swim. _Ryan said, "I would like to go for a swim."_

8. Parker replied no, I have not seen your lunch box. _Parker replied, "No, I have not seen your lunchbox._

Ask your child to listen to a short conversation between two family members and write it down using correct punctuation. If needed, ask the people to speak slowly so your child has time to write.

Subject-Verb Agreement

The **verb** in the predicate of a sentence must **agree** with the **subject** of a sentence. A **singular verb** has a **singular subject**. A **plural verb** has a **plural subject**.

If the subject is singular, add **s** or **es** to most present tense verbs. Remember, if the subject is a collective noun that is used as a unit, it is considered singular.

Example: Our <u>community</u> <u>has</u> a rowboat race every Fourth of July.

Write the verb that agrees with the subject of each sentence.

1. People _____ various kinds of watercraft for pleasure. (use, uses)

2. Old-fashioned muscle power _____ some types of watercraft. (propel, propels)

3. Some rafts _____ made by tying pieces of wood together. (is, are)

4. Pacific Islanders _____ out tree trunks to make dugout canoes. (digs, dig)

5. The world's largest dugout canoe _____ 70 people. (carry, carries)

6. Boys and girls often _____ canoeing at summer camps. (enjoy, enjoys)

7. One paddler _____ a type of canoe called a kayak. (steer, steers)

8. The paddle _____ double-bladed. (is, are)

9. Rowboats _____ usually heavier and wider than canoes. (is, are)

10. The rower _____ on two oars to steer the boat. (pull, pulls)

11. Rowboats _____ not tip over as easily as canoes. (do, does)

12. Adults and children often _____ from rowboats on lakes and rivers. (fish, fishes)

13. People _____ special lightweight, narrow rowboats called shells. (race, races)

Helping at Home

Have your child pretend to race to a finish line in slow motion while you read sentences with correct and incorrect subject/verb agreement. Each time your child hears a sentence with incorrect agreement, he or she must freeze for 10 seconds.

Possessive Nouns

A **possessive noun** is a word that shows who or what has something or owns something. Add an apostrophe and **s** (**'s**) to most common and proper singular nouns to show possession.

> **Examples:** girl/girl's, Olivia/Olivia's

Add an apostrophe (') to most common and proper plural nouns to show possession.

> **Examples:** mountains/ mountains', Alps/Alps'

Add an apostrophe and **s** (**'s**) to irregular plural nouns to show possession.

> **Example:** women/women's

Write the possessive form of each noun.

1. teachers ___teachers'___
2. teeth ___teeth's___
3. bracelet ___bracelet's___
4. galaxy ___galaxy's___
5. men ___men's___
6. T. rex ___T. rex's___
7. Tess ___Tess___
8. children ___children's___
9. industries ___industries'___
10. students ___students'___
11. meadow ___meadow's___
12. tennis ___tennis's___
13. Tuesday ___Tuesday's___
14. countesses ___countesses___

Rewrite each phrase using the possessive form of each bold noun.
Example: the shoe belonging to **Mel**/Mel's shoe

15. the flavor of the **french fries** ___the french fries' flavor___
16. the economy of **Canada** ___Canada's economy___
17. the cheers of the **crowd** ___the crowd's cheers___
18. the aroma of the **pies** ___the pies' aroma___

Helping at Home

Provide self-stick notes for your child to stick on objects around the house that belong to different family members. On each, have him or her write possessive nouns such as *dad's shoes*.

Exact Nouns and Verbs

An **exact noun** makes the meaning of a sentence more specific and more interesting.

> **Example:** Some <u>people</u> played a <u>game</u>./Some <u>boys</u> played <u>football</u>. (The noun <u>boys</u> tells who played, and the noun <u>football</u> tells what game was played. The meaning of the sentence is much more specific.)

An **exact verb** makes the meaning of a sentence more specific and more interesting.

> **Example:** Tyrone <u>scored</u>./Tyrone <u>kicked</u> a field goal. (The verb <u>kicked</u> gives a more specific picture of how Tyrone scored points.)

Underline the noun or verb in parentheses that makes the meaning of each sentence more specific and more interesting.

1. The (group, team) lined up on the field.

2. The (quarterback, boy) called the play.

3. He (passed, gave) the ball to the running back.

4. Marshall (ran, sprinted) up the field.

5. (People, Fans) cheered as Marshall gained another first down.

6. The (referee, man) signaled for a time-out.

7. The (kids, Bobcats) ran to the sidelines.

8. The (coaches, men) reviewed the game plan.

9. The two teams (returned, went) to the field.

10. The Bobcats' (quarterback, player) threw a pass for a touchdown.

11. It (made, tied) the score at 12-12!

12. The people in the (seats, stands) went wild!

Helping at Home

Have your child write a story about a sporting event he or she played in or watched. Read the story together and circle words that could be more specific and interesting. Try reading the story out loud with new, more exact words to see if it is improved.

Common Core State Standards for Math*

The following parent-friendly explanations of third grade Common Core math standards are provided to help you understand what your child will learn in school this year. Practice pages listed will help your child master each skill.

Complete Common Core State Standards may be found here: www.corestandards.org.

3.OA Operations and Algebraic Thinking

Represent and solve problems involving multiplication and division.
(Standards 3.OA.A.1, 3.OA.A.2, 3.OA.A.3, 3.OA.A.4)

Your child will multiply to figure out the total number of objects in equal groups and divide a set of objects into equal groups by using drawings and pictures.
• **Practice pages: 68–71, 76**

Your child will use multiplication and division within 100 to solve word problems.
• **Practice pages: 72, 73**

Your child will find missing numbers in multiplication and division problems. For example, he or she will find the number that is missing in equations like these: $5 = 15 \div ?$ or $? \times 8 = 64$.
• **Practice pages: 74, 75**

Understand properties of multiplication and the
relationship between multiplication and division.
(Standards 3.OA.B.5, 3.OA.B.6)

Your child will use the commutative property of multiplication (if $6 \times 4 = 24$, then $4 \times 6 = 24$), the associative property of multiplication ($3 \times 5 \times 2$ can be solved by multiplying $3 \times 5 = 15$, then $15 \times 2 = 30$ or by multiplying $5 \times 2 = 10$, then $3 \times 10 = 30$), and the distributive property of multiplication (8×15 can be changed to $8 \times (10 + 5)$; multiply (8×10) and (8×5) and add the products together: $80 + 40 = 120$). • **Practice pages: 76–78**

Your child will use multiplication to help understand division problems. For example, $32 \div 8$ can be solved by finding the number that makes 32 when multiplied by 8 (Answer: 4).
• **Practice pages: 74, 79**

Multiply and divide within 100.
(Standard 3.OA.C.7)

Your child will multiply and divide within 100 and memorize all the products of two one-digit numbers. • **Practice pages: 80, 81**

Solve problems involving the four operations,
and identify and explain patterns in arithmetic.
(Standards 3.OA.D.8, 3.OA.D.9)

Your child will solve two-step word problems using addition, subtraction, multiplication, and division. • **Practice pages: 82, 83**

Your child will find and explain patterns in multiplication and division tables.
• **Practice page: 75**

3.NBT Number and Operations in Base Ten

Use place value understanding and properties of
operations to perform multi-digit arithmetic.
(Standards 3.NBT.A.1, 3.NBT.A.2, 3.NBT.A.3)

Your child will round numbers to the nearest ten or hundred. • **Practice pages: 84, 85**

Your child will add and subtract within 1000 using place value and the relationship between addition and subtraction. • **Practice pages: 86, 87**

Your child will use place value to easily multiply one-digit numbers by multiples of 10. For example, $10 \times 2 = 20$ can be found by knowing $1 \times 2 = 2$ and adding 0 to the end.
• **Practice page: 88**

3.NF Number and Operations—Fractions

Develop understanding of fractions as numbers.
(Standards 3.NF.A.1, 3.NF.A.2a, 3.NF.A.2b, 3.NF.A.3a, 3.NF.A.3b, 3.NF.A.3c, 3.NF.A.3d)

Your child will see fractions as parts of a whole and understand the difference between numerators and denominators. • **Practice pages: 89, 90**

Your child will label fractions on a number line and divide a number line into equal parts to represent a fraction. • **Practice pages: 91, 93, 95**

Common Core State Standards for Math*

Your child will identify and form equivalent fractions and compare two fractions using <, >, and =. • **Practice pages: 96–102**

3.MD Measurement and Data

Solve problems involving measurement and estimation.
(Standards 3.MD.A.1, 3.MD.A.2)

Your child will tell and write time to the nearest minute and solve word problems in which he or she must add or subtract minutes. • **Practice pages: 103, 104**

Your child will measure volume and mass using grams (g), kilograms (kg), and liters (l) and solve word problems involving mass or volume. • **Practice pages: 105, 106**

Represent and interpret data.
(Standards 3.MD.B.3, 3.MD.B.4)

Your child will read bar graphs and picture graphs and answer questions using the information. • **Practice pages: 107, 108**

Your child will use rulers to measure in inches, half inches, and quarter inches and show the data on a line plot. • **Practice pages: 109, 110**

Geometric measurement: understand concepts of area
and relate area to multiplication and to addition.
(Standards 3.MD.C.5a, 3.MD.C.5b, 3.MD.C.6,
3.MD.C.7a, 3.MD.C.7b, 3.MD.C.7d)

Your child will find area by counting square units. • **Practice pages: 111, 112**

Your child will multiply a rectangle's length by its width to find its area. Your child will find the area of complex shapes by dividing them into smaller rectangles and adding the areas together. • **Practice pages: 113, 114, 116**

Geometric measurement: recognize perimeter as an attribute of
plane figures and distinguish between linear and area measures.
(Standard 3.MD.D.8)

Your child will add the lengths of a figure's sides together to find the perimeter.
• **Practice pages: 115, 116**

3.G Geometry

Reason with shapes and their attributes.
(Standards 3.G.A.1, 3.G.A.2)

Your child will identify, draw, and describe polygons based on attributes such as number of
sides. • **Practice pages: 117–119**

Your child will divide shapes into equal parts and use fractions to describe the parts.
• **Practice pages: 120, 121**

Multiplication

Draw a line from each multiplication problem to the way to say it. Then, draw a line to the matching picture.

1. 3 × 2 = _____   4 groups of 2

2. 2 × 5 = _____   3 groups of 4

3. 4 × 2 = _____   3 groups of 2

4. 3 × 4 = _____   2 groups of 5

5. 4 × 5 = _____   5 groups of 5

6   5 × 5 = _____   4 groups of 5

Draw groups of pictures to show each problem.

7. 4 × 4 = _____   8. 3 × 3 = _____

Helping at Home

Give your child an assortment of buttons, paperclips, or pennies. Write a multiplication problem on a piece of paper and have him or her use the items to visualize the problem, then solve.

Multiplication Word Problems

Write a word problem to match each description. Solve the problem. Draw a picture and write the equation.

1. 7 groups of 3

_____

_____

_____

_____

2. 6 groups of 5

_____

_____

_____

_____

3. 4 groups of 9

_____

_____

_____

_____

4. 12 groups of 6

_____

_____

_____

_____

Helping at Home

Ask your child to help you make dinner. While cooking, create multiplication word problems together such as, "If we have four people eating dinner tonight, and each one wants three rolls, how many rolls should we make?"

Division

Solve each problem.

Example: 20 ÷ 4
Draw a picture:

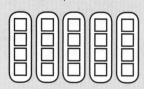

How many 4s are in 20? __5__
Subtract down:
20 – 4 = __16__   16 – 4 = __12__   12 – 4 = __8__
8 – 4 = __4__   4 – 4 = __0__

1. 21 ÷ 3
   How many 3s are in 21? _____

   Draw a picture. Subtract down.

2. 30 ÷ 5
   How many 5s are in 30? _____

   Draw a picture. Subtract down.

3. 36 ÷ 9
   How many 9s are in 36? _____

   Draw a picture. Subtract down.

4. 18 ÷ 6
   How many 6s are in 18? _____

   Draw a picture. Subtract down.

Division Word Problems

Write a word problem to match each description. Solve the problem. Draw a picture and write the equation.

1. 21 divided into 7 groups

2. 45 divided into 5 groups

3. 36 divided into 6 groups

4. 18 divided into 2 groups

Helping at Home

Have your child write more division word problems starring your child and his or her friends. Encourage your child to act out the word problems with his or her friends and solve them together.

Word Problems

Solve each problem. Draw a picture in the box to help you. Write your answer on the line.

1. Randy had 6 bags. He placed 9 marbles in each bag. How many marbles did he have?

2. Taron has 4 stacks of cards with 8 cards in each stack. How many cards does he have?

3. Jennifer jumped over 5 rocks. She jumped over each rock 9 times. How many times did she jump?

4. Zach runs 6 miles, 5 days a week. How many miles does he run in a week?

5. The skaters skated in 7 groups with 4 in each group. How many skaters were present in all of the groups?

6. Eight children went for a hike. Each child carried a backpack with 6 bandages in it. How many total bandages did they have?

For five days, time your child dribbling a basketball, jumping rope, or doing another activity. Write down the number of minutes each day. At the end of five days, ask your child to calculate the total number of minutes.

Helping at Home

© Carson-Dellosa • CD-704503

Word Problems

Draw an array to help you solve a multiplication problem. Then, count the number of marks you made.

3 × 5 = ___15___

Solve each problem. Draw an array in the box to help you. Write your answer on the line.

1. The store display had 9 shelves. The stock boy placed 9 boxes of cereal on each shelf. How many boxes of cereal were on display?

2. The third graders formed 8 relay teams. Seven students were on each team. How many students were running the relay?

3. Ms. Martinez made a scrapbook for her daughter. The scrapbook had 7 pages. Each page had 6 pictures. How many pictures were in the scrapbook?

4. John keeps his baseball cards in a notebook. His notebook has 8 pages. Each page has 9 cards. How many cards does John have?

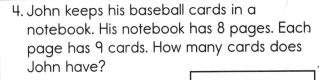

5. Jenna wrote 2 pages in her diary each day of the week. How many pages did she write each week?

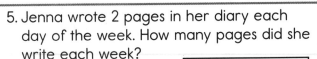

6. Carlos has 5 jars of marbles. He has 8 marbles in each jar. How many marbles does he have?

Helping at Home

Bake cookies with your child. Arrange the cookies in an array and ask your child to write the matching multiplication problem and solve it. Allow your child to arrange arrays for you to solve. Then, enjoy a snack together.

Multiplication and Division

Find each missing number.

1. $3 \times \underline{9} = 27$ $7 \times \underline{6} = 42$ $5 \times \underline{10} = 50$ $12 \times \underline{3} = 36$

2. $\underline{7} \times 7 = 49$ $9 \times \underline{9} = 81$ $4 \times \underline{7} = 28$ $\underline{3} \times 8 = 32$

3. $\underline{9} \times 5 = 45$ $\underline{3} \times 4 = 12$ $\underline{9} \times 8 = 72$ $6 \times \underline{4} = 24$

4. $\underline{8} \times 8 = 64$ $6 \times \underline{8} = 48$ $\underline{9} \times 7 = 63$ $10 \times \underline{10} = 100$

5. $6 \times \underline{7} = 42$ $\underline{4} \times 4 = 16$ $8 \times \underline{5} = 40$ $\underline{7} \times 3 = 21$

Find each missing number. Use a multiplication fact to help you.

6. $48 \div \boxed{6} = 8$ $36 \div \boxed{6} = 6$ $36 \div \boxed{9} = 4$

7. $\boxed{42} \div 7 = 6$ $\boxed{45} \div 9 = 5$ $\boxed{28} \div 4 = 7$

8. $\boxed{80} \div 10 = 8$ $63 \div \boxed{7} = 9$ $27 \div \boxed{9} = 3$

9. $5 = 15 \div \boxed{}$ $6 = \boxed{} \div 5$ $10 = \boxed{} \div 3$

10. $22 = 44 \div \boxed{}$ $7 = \boxed{1} \div 7$ $7 = 56 \div \boxed{8}$

Finding Patterns

Look at each pattern. Complete the chart.

1.

Rule: × 2	
2	4
3	6
4	8
5	10
6	12
7	14

2.

Rule: ÷ 3	
12	4
21	7
30	10
15	5
60	
24	

3.

Rule: × 5	
2	10
3	15
4	20
5	25
6	30
7	35

4.

Rule: ÷ 4	
40	10
32	8
4	1
44	11
36	9
28	7

5.

Rule: × 4	
2	8
3	12
4	16
5	20
6	24
7	28

6.

Rule: ÷ 5	
20	4
35	7
40	8
15	3
5	1
10	2

Use sidewalk chalk to create number patterns outside. Encourage your child to make a pattern and challenge you to find the rule.

Commutative Property of Multiplication

Use the pictures to represent each problem. Solve the problem.

Example: $2 \times 3 = 6, 3 \times 2 = 6$

1. ____ × ____ = __2__   ____ × ____ = __8__

2. ____ × ____ = ____   ____ × ____ = ____

3. ____ × ____ = ____   ____ × ____ = __1__

4. __3__ × ____ = __15__   ____ × ____ = ____

5. ____ × __3__ = ____   ____ × __2__ = __0__

6. ____ × ____ = ____   ____ × __4__ = __13__

Draw a picture to match each problem. Solve the problem.

7. 6 × 4 = _____   8. 5 × 6 = _____

9. 2 × 7 = _____   10. 8 × 2 = _____

11. 3 × 8 = _____   12. 2 × 9 = _____

Complete each equation.

13. 8 × 3 = 3 × _____   14. 5 × 4 = 4 × _____

15. 7 × 2 = _____ × 7   16. 4 × 3 = _____ × 4

While driving in the car, practice mental math with your child. Ask, "What is 2 × 3?" If your child answers correctly, switch the order of the problem to practice the commutative property by asking, "What is 3 × 2?"

Helping at Home

Associative Property of Multiplication

Use the associative property to solve each problem in two different ways.

Example:

3 × 5 × 2   (3 × 5) × 2 =   3 × (5 × 2) =
                  15 × 2 = 30   3 × 10 = 30

1. 2 × 6 × 1 = 12	2. 9 × 10 × 1 = 90
3. 7 × 4 × 3 =	4. 8 × 3 × 2 = 48
5. 10 × 5 × 4 =	6. 3 × 4 × 2 =
7. 4 × 2 × 5 =	8. 2 × 10 × 3 =

Helping at Home

Write the numbers 1 through 9 on separate index cards and put them into a bag. Have your child draw three numbers and create a multiplication equation. Ask your child to use the associative property to solve it two different ways.

Distributive Property

The **distributive property** can make multiplying large numbers easier.

8 × 15 = ?   Think: How can I make this factor smaller?
8 × (10 + 5)
(8 × 10) + (8 × 5)
80 + 40 = 120

Use the distributive property to solve each problem.

1. 7 x 8 = [56]

7 × (__4__ + __4__)

(7 × __4__) + (7 × __4__)

__28__ + __28__ = 56

2. 3 × 17 = [51]

3 × (__9__ + __4__)

(3 × __8__) + (3 × __9__)

__24__ + __27__ = 51

3. 22 × 5 = [110]

4. 4 × 18 = [ ]

5. 6 × 13 = [ ]

6. 7 × 12 = [ ]

Division

A **dividend** is the number being divided. A **divisor** is the number by which the dividend is divided. A **quotient** is the answer to a division problem.

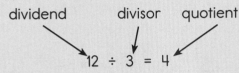

dividend   divisor   quotient

$12 \div 3 = 4$

divisor ← quotient
$3\overline{)12}$ ← dividend

Knowing how to multiply can help you divide. Ask yourself: What number multiplied by the divisor equals the dividend? 3 x _____ = 12   3 x 4 = 12

Divide. Write the multiplication fact that helped you. Then, match the quotients to the numbers below and fill in the correct letters.

W	T	I	F
1. $7\overline{)42}$	2. $9\overline{)9}$	3. $6\overline{)30}$	4. $5\overline{)40}$
A	**S**	**L**	**R**
5. $8\overline{)56}$	6. $3\overline{)27}$	7. $8\overline{)80}$	8. $8\overline{)16}$
	K	**E**	
	9. $9\overline{)36}$	10. $7\overline{)21}$	

The first bicycles had no pedals. People walked them along until they came to a hill. Then, they rode down the hill.

What was the first bicycle called?

A S W I F I V A L K E R
7 9 6 5 8 1 6 7 10 4 3 2

© Carson-Dellosa • CD-704503

Helping at Home

Use division to tell your child a funny joke every day. Make a key like the one on this page and have your child solve problems to find the punch line to the joke.

Multiplication

Solve each problem.

1. 6 × 5 = __30__   7 × 7 = __49__   9 × 3 = __27__   4 × 8 = __32__

2. 5 × 9 = __45__   6 × 3 = __18__   7 × 6 = __42__   9 × 5 = __49__

3. 9 × 9 = __81__   8 × 3 = __24__   3 × 7 = __21__   4 × 9 = __36__

4. 8 × 7 = __56__   9 × 6 = __54__   6 × 6 = __36__   8 × 8 = __64__

5.
$$\begin{array}{r} 2 \\ \times\,4 \\ \hline 8 \end{array}$$
$$\begin{array}{r} 10 \\ \times\,6 \\ \hline 60 \end{array}$$
$$\begin{array}{r} 5 \\ \times\,3 \\ \hline 15 \end{array}$$
$$\begin{array}{r} 3 \\ \times\,6 \\ \hline 18 \end{array}$$
$$\begin{array}{r} 11 \\ \times\,5 \\ \hline 55 \end{array}$$
$$\begin{array}{r} 4 \\ \times\,7 \\ \hline 28 \end{array}$$
$$\begin{array}{r} 6 \\ \times\,4 \\ \hline 24 \end{array}$$

6.
$$\begin{array}{r} 2 \\ \times\,3 \\ \hline 6 \end{array}$$
$$\begin{array}{r} 7 \\ \times\,5 \\ \hline 35 \end{array}$$
$$\begin{array}{r} 2 \\ \times\,9 \\ \hline 18 \end{array}$$
$$\begin{array}{r} 3 \\ \times\,8 \\ \hline 24 \end{array}$$
$$\begin{array}{r} 8 \\ \times\,4 \\ \hline 32 \end{array}$$
$$\begin{array}{r} 2 \\ \times\,5 \\ \hline 10 \end{array}$$
$$\begin{array}{r} 9 \\ \times\,3 \\ \hline 27 \end{array}$$

7.
$$\begin{array}{r} 4 \\ \times\,4 \\ \hline 16 \end{array}$$
$$\begin{array}{r} 3 \\ \times\,3 \\ \hline 9 \end{array}$$
$$\begin{array}{r} 9 \\ \times\,5 \\ \hline 45 \end{array}$$
$$\begin{array}{r} 3 \\ \times\,4 \\ \hline 12 \end{array}$$
$$\begin{array}{r} 7 \\ \times\,6 \\ \hline 42 \end{array}$$
$$\begin{array}{r} 5 \\ \times\,6 \\ \hline 30 \end{array}$$
$$\begin{array}{r} 6 \\ \times\,8 \\ \hline 48 \end{array}$$

8.
$$\begin{array}{r} 6 \\ \times\,6 \\ \hline 36 \end{array}$$
$$\begin{array}{r} 9 \\ \times\,7 \\ \hline 63 \end{array}$$
$$\begin{array}{r} 8 \\ \times\,7 \\ \hline 56 \end{array}$$
$$\begin{array}{r} 8 \\ \times\,5 \\ \hline 40 \end{array}$$
$$\begin{array}{r} 4 \\ \times\,9 \\ \hline 36 \end{array}$$
$$\begin{array}{r} 4 \\ \times\,8 \\ \hline 32 \end{array}$$
$$\begin{array}{r} 7 \\ \times\,7 \\ \hline 49 \end{array}$$

9. 5 × 5 = __25__   4 × 7 = __28__   8 × 9 = __72__   2 × 7 = __14__

Helping at Home

Ask your child to turn each multiplication problem on this page into a division equation. Discuss the relationship between multiplication and division with your child.

Division

Solve each problem. Draw a picture if it helps you find the answer.

Example:

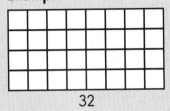

32

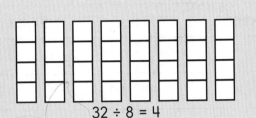

$32 \div 8 = 4$

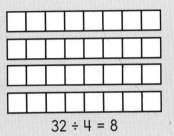

$32 \div 4 = 8$

1. $6 \div 2 = \underline{3}$

   $6 \div 3 = \underline{2}$

2. $12 \div 3 = \underline{4}$

   $12 \div 4 = \underline{3}$

3. $15 \div 5 = \underline{3}$

   $15 \div 3 = \underline{5}$

4. $10 \div 5 = \underline{2}$

   $10 \div 2 = \underline{5}$

5. $16 \div 2 = \underline{8}$

   $16 \div 8 = \underline{2}$

6. $20 \div 4 = \underline{5}$

   $20 \div 5 = \underline{4}$

7. $24 \div 6 = \underline{4}$

   $24 \div 4 = \underline{6}$

8. $28 \div 4 = \underline{7}$

   $28 \div 7 = \underline{4}$

9. $36 \div 9 = \underline{4}$

   $36 \div 4 = \underline{9}$

10. $16 \div 8 = \underline{2}$

    $16 \div 2 = \underline{8}$

11. $48 \div 6 = \underline{8}$

    $48 \div 8 = \underline{6}$

12. $54 \div 9 = \underline{6}$

    $54 \div 6 = \underline{9}$

Shown below is another way to write division problems. Solve each problem.

13. $5\overline{)40}$ $\quad$ 8

14. $6\overline{)42}$ $\quad$ 7

15. $3\overline{)27}$ $\quad$ 9

16. $2\overline{)16}$ $\quad$ 8

17. $7\overline{)49}$ $\quad$ 7

18. $8\overline{)56}$ $\quad$ 7

19. $4\overline{)16}$ $\quad$ 4

20. $9\overline{)45}$ $\quad$ 5

21. $10\overline{)90}$ $\quad$ 9

22. $6\overline{)48}$ $\quad$ 8

23. $7\overline{)56}$ $\quad$ 8

24. $9\overline{)36}$ $\quad$ 7

Helping at Home

For any incorrect answers on this page, encourage your child to draw a picture to help him or her find the correct answer. For all correct answers, have your child write a multiplication problem that helped him or her solve the problem.

Two-Step Word Problems

Use the table to answer each question.

Sam's Market

Fruit	Price
cherries	$2.99 per lb.
apples	$0.89 per lb.
grapes	$1.49 per lb.
strawberries	$3.49 per basket
bananas	$0.59 per lb.
pineapples	$1.99 each

1. Jose wants to buy 1 pound of grapes and 1 pineapple. He has $5.00. Can he purchase these two items? Explain.

   he could buy both of them. answer: $3.48

2. Jeremy needs 1 basket of strawberries, 1 pineapple, and 1 pound of cherries to make a fruit salad. If he pays with a $10.00 bill, will he get change back? Explain.

   Yes! cause all the fruit cost $6.97 but he has $10.00, so he would get change $6.97

3. Andy has 6 quarters. Does he have enough money to buy 1 pineapple? Explain.

   4 quart. = $1.00   2 quart. = 50¢   no. cause he h $1.50 but a pin

4. Anna had $10.00. She bought 3 pounds of fruit. She got $5.53 in change. What fruit did she buy? Explain.

   grapes cause you

Two-Step Word Problems

Solve each problem.

1. Kristin made half as many sundaes as Reese. If they made 30 sundaes in all, how many did Kristin make?

15   sundaes.

2. Chang has 36 dog bones. He has 5 dogs. If he buys 4 more bones, how many bones will each dog get?

9   bones

3. Alex has 11 apples. He needs 5 apples to make 1 pie. If he has to make 5 pies, how many more apples does he need?

$$\begin{array}{r} \overline{20} \\ -\ 11 \\ \hline 14 \end{array}$$

14 more apples.

4. Upton and Nassim were playing basketball. Upton won twice as many times as he lost. He won 14 games. How many games did the boys play?

28 games

5. Jenny has 19 walnuts. She wants to divide them evenly into 4 bags. If she eats 3 walnuts, how many will she put into each bag?

ple costs $1.99.

4   walnuts.

6. Mom bought 15 cookies for dessert. There are 4 people in the family. How many cookies will each person get? How many will be left over?

3 cookies and 3 left.

Helping at Home

Have your child think out loud while he or she solves each problem on this page. Let your child reason through the steps to solve the problem and encourage him or her to write down and show his or her work.

Rounding: Tens

When **rounding** to the nearest ten, follow these steps:
1. Look at the ones place.
2. If the digit is 0, 1, 2, 3, or 4, round down.
3. If the digit is 5, 6, 7, 8, or 9, round up.

Examples: 3<u>4</u> rounds down to 30.
3<u>7</u> rounds up to 40.

Round to the nearest ten.

1. 39 _____
2. 62 _____
3. 55 _____
4. 93 _____
5. 74 _____

6. 33 _____
7. 26 _____
8. 41 _____
9. 24 _____
10. 38 _____

11. 296 _____
12. 989 _____
13. 458 _____
14. 434 _____
15. 692 _____

16. 916 _____
17. 776 _____
18. 381 _____
19. 252 _____
20. 722 _____

21. Mariah ate 21 almonds and 17 peanuts. About how many nuts did she eat in all?

22. Meg had 97 stamps. Tony had 83 stamps. About how many more stamps did Meg have than Tony?

Look for numbers around your house or around your community. They may include addresses, weights, or numbers on license plates. Encourage your child to round each number to the nearest ten.

Rounding: Hundreds

When **rounding** to the nearest hundred, follow these steps:
1. Look at the tens place.
2. If the digit is 1, 2, 3, or 4, round down.
3. If the digit is 5, 6, 7, 8, or 9, round up.

Examples: 7<u>4</u>4 rounds down to 700.
7<u>8</u>2 rounds up to 800.

Round the amount in each treasure chest to the nearest hundred.

1.
$692
$ _____

2.
$140
$ _____

3.
$569
$ _____

4.
$303
$ _____

5.
$684
$ _____

6.
$851
$ _____

7.
$712
$ _____

8.
$476
$ _____

9.
$925
$ _____

Helping at Home

Have your child roll a die three times and write each number rolled as one digit of a three-digit number. Then, have your child round the number to the nearest hundred.

Addition and Subtraction

Solve each problem.

1.
$$\begin{array}{r} 34 \\ +15 \\ \hline \end{array}\qquad \begin{array}{r} 28 \\ +31 \\ \hline \end{array}\qquad \begin{array}{r} 81 \\ +17 \\ \hline \end{array}\qquad \begin{array}{r} 54 \\ +35 \\ \hline \end{array}\qquad \begin{array}{r} 84 \\ +12 \\ \hline \end{array}\qquad \begin{array}{r} 17 \\ +32 \\ \hline \end{array}$$

2.
$$\begin{array}{r} 51 \\ +22 \\ \hline \end{array}\qquad \begin{array}{r} 73 \\ +14 \\ \hline \end{array}\qquad \begin{array}{r} 14 \\ +13 \\ \hline \end{array}\qquad \begin{array}{r} 20 \\ +48 \\ \hline \end{array}\qquad \begin{array}{r} 41 \\ +54 \\ \hline \end{array}\qquad \begin{array}{r} 36 \\ +21 \\ \hline \end{array}$$

3.
$$\begin{array}{r} 86 \\ -32 \\ \hline \end{array}\qquad \begin{array}{r} 52 \\ -12 \\ \hline \end{array}\qquad \begin{array}{r} 67 \\ -45 \\ \hline \end{array}\qquad \begin{array}{r} 95 \\ -30 \\ \hline \end{array}\qquad \begin{array}{r} 87 \\ -26 \\ \hline \end{array}\qquad \begin{array}{r} 48 \\ -33 \\ \hline \end{array}$$

4.
$$\begin{array}{r} 39 \\ -13 \\ \hline \end{array}\qquad \begin{array}{r} 66 \\ -46 \\ \hline \end{array}\qquad \begin{array}{r} 38 \\ -14 \\ \hline \end{array}\qquad \begin{array}{r} 75 \\ -52 \\ \hline \end{array}\qquad \begin{array}{r} 88 \\ -37 \\ \hline \end{array}\qquad \begin{array}{r} 74 \\ -24 \\ \hline \end{array}$$

5.
$$\begin{array}{r} 182 \\ +703 \\ \hline \end{array}\qquad \begin{array}{r} 231 \\ +547 \\ \hline \end{array}\qquad \begin{array}{r} 825 \\ +163 \\ \hline \end{array}\qquad \begin{array}{r} 436 \\ +562 \\ \hline \end{array}\qquad \begin{array}{r} 325 \\ +202 \\ \hline \end{array}$$

6.
$$\begin{array}{r} 274 \\ +320 \\ \hline \end{array}\qquad \begin{array}{r} 641 \\ +345 \\ \hline \end{array}\qquad \begin{array}{r} 908 \\ +\ 61 \\ \hline \end{array}\qquad \begin{array}{r} 365 \\ +424 \\ \hline \end{array}\qquad \begin{array}{r} 207 \\ +712 \\ \hline \end{array}$$

7.
$$\begin{array}{r} 684 \\ -253 \\ \hline \end{array}\qquad \begin{array}{r} 634 \\ -421 \\ \hline \end{array}\qquad \begin{array}{r} 835 \\ -610 \\ \hline \end{array}\qquad \begin{array}{r} 738 \\ -502 \\ \hline \end{array}\qquad \begin{array}{r} 325 \\ -102 \\ \hline \end{array}$$

Helping at Home

Ask your child how he or she solved several of the problems on this page. For instance, was place value used to break the problem down or did your child use the relationship between addition and subtraction to solve?

Addition and Subtraction

Solve each problem by regrouping.

1.
$$27 + 24 = 51$$
$$39 + 53 = \text{?}$$
$$46 + 35 = \text{?}$$
$$57 + 29 = \text{?}$$
$$49 + 15 = 64$$
$$63 + 27 = \text{?}$$

2.
$$75 + 19 = 44$$
$$93 + 37 = \text{?}$$
$$58 + 34 = \text{?}$$
$$64 + 28 = 92$$
$$86 + 17 = \text{?}$$
$$74 + 28 = \text{?}$$

3.
$$36 - 17 = \text{?}$$
$$98 - 19 = \text{?}$$
$$28 - 9 = \text{?}$$
$$41 - 15 = \text{?}$$
$$33 - 17 = \text{?}$$
$$67 - 18 = 44$$

4.
$$72 - 53 = \text{?}$$
$$85 - 27 = \text{?}$$
$$43 - 29 = \text{?}$$
$$96 - 37 = 59$$
$$64 - 36 = \text{?}$$
$$50 - 18 = \text{?}$$

5.
$$187 + 753 = \text{?}$$
$$263 + 347 = \text{?}$$
$$827 + 264 = \text{?}$$
$$726 + 585 = \text{?}$$
$$126 + 294 = \text{?}$$

6.
$$283 + 328 = \text{?}$$
$$268 + 345 = \text{?}$$
$$418 + 199 = \text{?}$$
$$385 + 826 = \text{?}$$
$$294 + 765 = \text{?}$$

7.
$$837 - 138 = \text{?}$$
$$516 - 247 = \text{?}$$
$$825 - 356 = \text{?}$$
$$713 - 284 = \text{?}$$
$$624 - 367 = \text{?}$$

Helping at Home

Ask your child to check each addition problem on this page using subtraction and to check each subtraction problem using addition. If any of the answers do not agree, have your child attempt the original problem again.

Multiplication by 10

Look for a pattern to help multiply numbers by 10. Any whole number times 10 is that number with a 0 added at the end. Finding the pattern helps you do these in your head.

$$\begin{array}{r} 10 \\ \times\ 2 \\ \hline \mathbf{20} \end{array} \qquad \begin{array}{r} 10 \\ \times\ 3 \\ \hline \mathbf{30} \end{array}$$

Solve each problem.

1.
$$\begin{array}{r} 10 \\ \times\ 8 \\ \hline \end{array} \qquad \begin{array}{r} 10 \\ \times\ 7 \\ \hline \end{array} \qquad \begin{array}{r} 10 \\ \times\ 4 \\ \hline \end{array} \qquad \begin{array}{r} 10 \\ \times\ 9 \\ \hline \end{array} \qquad \begin{array}{r} 10 \\ \times\ 3 \\ \hline \end{array}$$

2.
$$\begin{array}{r} 10 \\ \times\ 6 \\ \hline \end{array} \qquad \begin{array}{r} 10 \\ \times\ 10 \\ \hline \end{array} \qquad \begin{array}{r} 10 \\ \times\ 2 \\ \hline \end{array} \qquad \begin{array}{r} 10 \\ \times\ 5 \\ \hline \end{array} \qquad \begin{array}{r} 10 \\ \times\ 3 \\ \hline \end{array}$$

Multiply 5 × 3.
Then, add a zero.

$$\begin{array}{r} 50 \\ \times\ 3 \\ \hline \end{array} \qquad \begin{array}{r} 50 \\ \times\ 3 \\ \hline 150 \end{array}$$

3.
$$\begin{array}{r} 20 \\ \times\ 2 \\ \hline \end{array} \qquad \begin{array}{r} 60 \\ \times\ 7 \\ \hline \end{array} \qquad \begin{array}{r} 20 \\ \times\ 3 \\ \hline \end{array} \qquad \begin{array}{r} 40 \\ \times\ 6 \\ \hline \end{array} \qquad \begin{array}{r} 90 \\ \times\ 9 \\ \hline \end{array}$$

4.
$$\begin{array}{r} 80 \\ \times\ 5 \\ \hline \end{array} \qquad \begin{array}{r} 30 \\ \times\ 4 \\ \hline \end{array} \qquad \begin{array}{r} 70 \\ \times\ 8 \\ \hline \end{array} \qquad \begin{array}{r} 60 \\ \times\ 5 \\ \hline \end{array} \qquad \begin{array}{r} 50 \\ \times\ 4 \\ \hline \end{array}$$

Helping at Home

Write the numbers 1 through 10 on separate index cards. Have your child fan out the cards and ask you to pick one. For the card you choose, have your child tell you the product when multiplied by 10.

Fractions

Cross out any shapes that are not divided into equal parts. Then, write the correct fraction for each remaining shape.

1.  $\frac{1}{3}$

2. 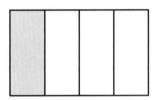 $\frac{1}{4}$

3. 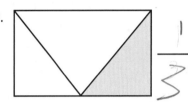 $\frac{1}{3}$

4.  $\frac{1}{3}$

5. $\frac{1}{6}$

6. 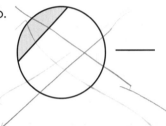 $\frac{}{}$

Answer each question.

7. Claire says that the following shape shows $\frac{1}{3}$. Wyatt says that it does not. Who is correct? Explain.

Wyatt is correct because the shape that is colored in is the odd one, & wyatt said it is not correct, so he is right

8. Kade was asked to draw $\frac{3}{4}$ in two different ways. Did he draw the fractions correctly? Explain.

He did because $\frac{3}{4}$ is equal shapes & so he did that.

Helping at Home

Cut a snack such as an apple or a slice of cheese into thirds, fourths, or fifths. As your child eats, ask him or her to name a fraction to describe how much is left.

Fractions

A **fraction** tells about equal parts of a whole. The top number tells how many parts are shaded. The bottom number tells how many parts in all.

Parts shaded ⟶ $\dfrac{1}{6}$

Parts in all ⟶

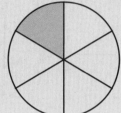

Write each fraction.

1.
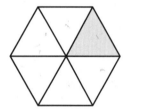
$\dfrac{11}{6}$

2.
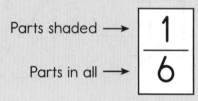
$\dfrac{3}{8}$

3.
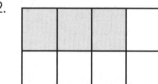
$\dfrac{1}{2}$

4.
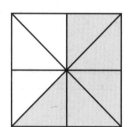
$\dfrac{45}{58}$

5.
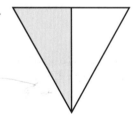
$\dfrac{10}{16}$

6.
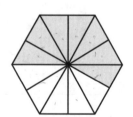
$\dfrac{7}{12}$

Helping at Home

Ask your child how the numerator would change if he or she shaded one more part in each shape on this page. Have your child explain why the denominator would stay the same.

Fractions on a Number Line

Cut out the fraction strips. Use them to help you label the number line.

Make sure the fraction strips start at 0. Make sure the intervals are equal.

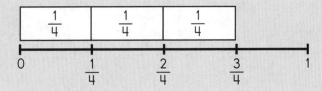

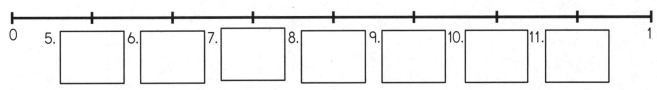

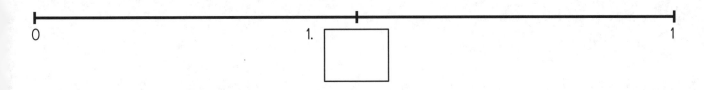

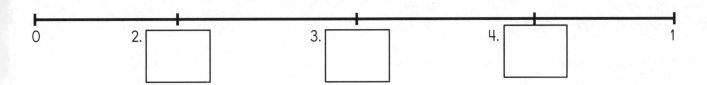

cut ✂

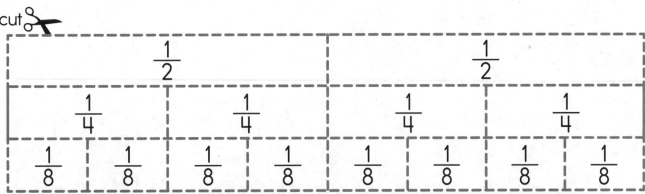

Use colorful tape to make a number line on your floor. Call out different fractions and ask your child to stand where the fraction would fall on the number line.

Helping at Home

Fractions on a Number Line

Mark and label each fraction on the number line. Use the fraction strips to help you.

Make sure the fraction strips start at 0. Make sure the intervals are equal.

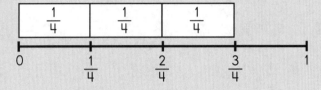

1. 0, $\frac{1}{2}$, 1

2. 0, $\frac{1}{4}$, $\frac{2}{4}$, $\frac{3}{4}$, 1

3. 0, $\frac{1}{8}$, $\frac{2}{8}$, $\frac{3}{8}$, $\frac{4}{8}$, $\frac{5}{8}$, $\frac{6}{8}$, $\frac{7}{8}$, 1

cut

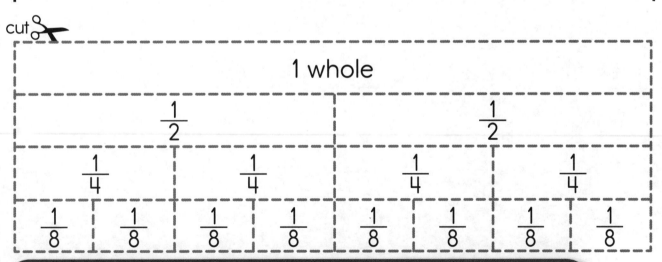

Helping at Home

Draw shapes and divide them into equal parts with your child. Encourage him or her to create a number line and plot matching fractions on the number line.

Fractions on a Number Line

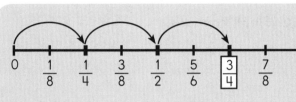

The denominator is the number of intervals in all.

The numerator is the number of intervals passed.

Label each number line.

1.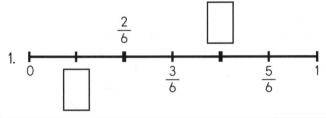

2.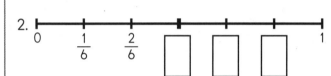

3.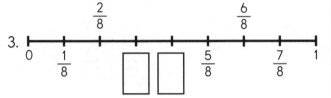

4.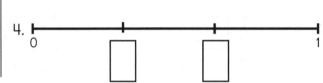

Label each number line with the fractions.

5. fourths and eighths

0   1

6. thirds and sixths

0   1

7. Explain how you know your number lines are correct.

_____

_____

Helping at Home

Use sidewalk chalk to draw a number line outside. Have your child stand on any fraction you name. Then, name a series of two or more fractions and have your child jump to the different fractions on the number line.

Equivalent Fractions

Fractions that equal the same amount are called **equivalent fractions**.

Example:

$$\frac{1}{2} = \frac{2}{4}$$

Write the equivalent fractions.

1.
$$\frac{1}{3} = \frac{2}{6}$$

2.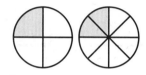
$$\frac{1}{4} = \frac{2}{8}$$

3.
$$\frac{1}{2} = \frac{3}{6}$$

4.
$$\frac{6}{8} = \frac{3}{4}$$

5.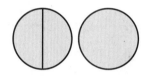
$$\frac{2}{2} = \frac{2}{4}$$

6.
$$\frac{3}{7} = \frac{1}{4}$$

7.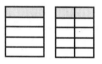
$$\frac{1}{5} = \frac{2}{10}$$

8.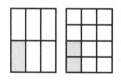
$$\underline{} = \frac{2}{12}$$

9.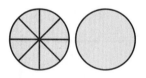
$$\frac{8}{8} = \frac{2}{3}$$

10.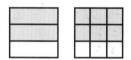
$$\frac{2}{3} = \frac{6}{1}$$

11.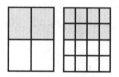
$$\frac{1}{4} = \frac{8}{16}$$

12.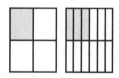
$$\frac{1}{4} = \frac{3}{12}$$

Help your child draw partitioned and shaded shapes and matching fractions on separate index cards. Turn the cards over and use them to play Memory.

© Carson-Dellosa • CD-704503

Equivalent Fractions

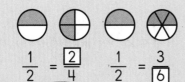

$\frac{1}{2} = \frac{\boxed{2}}{4}$ $\frac{1}{2} = \frac{3}{\boxed{6}}$

Equivalent fractions are fractions that are equal. Draw pictures to find equivalent fractions.

Draw a picture of each fraction. Write the missing numbers to show equivalent fractions.

1. $\frac{1}{3} = \frac{\boxed{}}{6}$

2. $\frac{1}{4} = \frac{\boxed{}}{8}$

3. $\frac{2}{3} = \frac{\boxed{}}{6}$

4. $\frac{3}{4} = \frac{6}{\boxed{}}$

5. $\frac{6}{8} = \frac{3}{\boxed{}}$

6. $\frac{4}{6} = \frac{\boxed{}}{3}$

7. $\frac{2}{4} = \frac{1}{\boxed{}}$

8. $\frac{1}{2} = \frac{\boxed{}}{4} = \frac{3}{\boxed{}} = \frac{\boxed{}}{8}$

Helping at Home
Have your child use construction paper and markers to create an equivalent fraction collage. See how many different ways your child can draw equivalent fractions for $\frac{1}{2}$. Display the completed artwork on the refrigerator or wall.

Equivalent Fractions

Solve each problem.

1. Explain how the number line shows equivalent fractions.

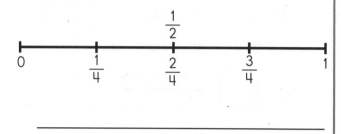

_____

_____

2. Complete the number line to show that $\frac{1}{3}$ and $\frac{2}{6}$ are equivalent.

```
0                                    1
```

3. Which fractions are equivalent?

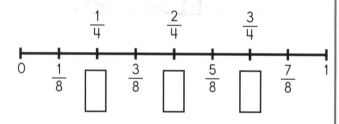

4. Which fractions are equivalent to 1 whole?

_____

Explain how you know they are equivalent.

_____

_____

_____

5. Juan says that $\frac{5}{8}$ and $\frac{1}{2}$ are equivalent.

Is he correct? Explain why or why not. Draw a number line to help you.

_____

_____

6. Tell what an equivalent fraction is in your own words.

_____

_____

_____

Whole Numbers as Fractions

Write each whole number as a fraction.

Example:

$$3 = \frac{12}{4}$$

1.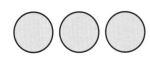

4 = ——

2.

2 = ——

3.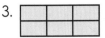

2 = ——

4.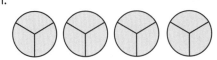

5 = ——

5.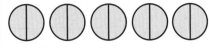

5 = ——

6.

4 = ——

7.

3 = ——

8.

4 = ——

9.

2 = ——

Draw a picture to show each number as a fraction. Then, write each whole number as a fraction.

10. 6	11. 3	12. 8
13. 10	14. 7	15. 9

 Helping at Home Have your child write his or her age as a whole number and as a fraction with a denominator of 12. Explain that since $\frac{1}{12}$ of a year is one month, the fraction shows your child's age in months. Can your child show the fraction in a drawing?

Whole Numbers as Fractions

Write each fraction as a whole number. Draw a picture to help you.

1. $\dfrac{12}{3}$ = __4__

2. $\dfrac{10}{2}$ = _____

3. $\dfrac{16}{4}$ = _____

4. $\dfrac{12}{2}$ = _____

5. $\dfrac{16}{8}$ = _____

6. $\dfrac{20}{4}$ = _____

7. $\dfrac{28}{4}$ = _____

8. $\dfrac{21}{3}$ = _____

9. $\dfrac{16}{2}$ = _____

10. $\dfrac{36}{4}$ = _____

11. $\dfrac{9}{3}$ = _____

12. $\dfrac{40}{8}$ = _____

13. $\dfrac{22}{2}$ = _____

14. $\dfrac{30}{3}$ = _____

Helping at Home

Have your child write each whole number on this page as a fraction with a different denominator than what is shown. For example, 4 could be $\frac{8}{2}$ or $\frac{32}{8}$.

Comparing Fractions

To compare fractions, determine which figure has more area shaded. If necessary, find equivalent fractions and compare the numerators.

$$\frac{1}{2} = \frac{3}{6}$$

$$\frac{1}{3} = \frac{2}{6}$$

$$\frac{1}{2} > \frac{1}{3}$$

$$\frac{3}{6} > \frac{2}{6}$$

Write the correct fractions. Then, write <, >, or = to compare each pair of fractions.

1.

_____ ◯ _____

2.

_____ ◯ _____

3.
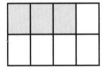

_____ _____

4.

_____ ◯ _____

5.

_____ _____

6.

_____ _____

Helping at Home

Ask your child to explain the thinking used to find the answers on this page. For example, did your child use the drawings or was it easier to find equivalent fractions? Talking through the process will help your child better understand it.

Comparing Fractions

Draw a picture of each fraction. Write >, <, or = to compare each pair of fractions.

1. $\frac{1}{3}$ ◯ $\frac{3}{3}$

2. $\frac{1}{4}$ ◯ $\frac{3}{4}$

3. $\frac{4}{6}$ ◯ $\frac{1}{6}$

4. $\frac{1}{2}$ ◯ $\frac{2}{2}$

5. $\frac{7}{8}$ ◯ $\frac{5}{8}$

6. $\frac{2}{4}$ ◯ $\frac{1}{4}$

7. Each pair of fractions above has the same denominator.

Complete this statement: If the denominators are the same, the fraction with the smaller numerator is _____ .

8. $\frac{2}{2}$ ◯ $\frac{2}{3}$

9. $\frac{1}{6}$ ◯ $\frac{1}{3}$

10. $\frac{4}{8}$ ◯ $\frac{4}{4}$

11. $\frac{1}{3}$ ◯ $\frac{1}{2}$

12. $\frac{3}{6}$ ◯ $\frac{3}{8}$

13. $\frac{5}{6}$ ◯ $\frac{5}{8}$

14. Each pair of fractions above has the same numerator.

Complete this statement: If the numerators are the same, the fraction with the smaller denominator is _____ .

Helping at Home Glue two toothpicks together to make < and > symbols. Use magnetic numbers and single toothpicks to create different fractions. Then, have your child place the correct < or > symbol between the fractions to compare.

Time

Use the time shown on each clock to answer the questions.

1.

What time does the clock show? __8:00__

What time would it be if it were 20 minutes earlier? __7:40__

What time will it be in 3 hours and 35 minutes? __11:35__

What time will it be in 65 minutes? __1:05__

2.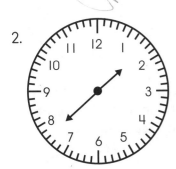

What time does the clock show? _____

What time would it be if it were 48 minutes earlier? _____

What time will it be in 5 hours and 22 minutes? _____

What time will it be in 57 minutes? _____

3.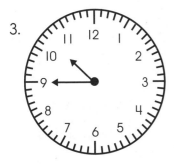

What time does the clock show? _____

What time would it be if it were 8 hours and 15 minutes earlier? _____

What time will it be in 4 hours and 15 minutes? _____

What time will it be in 75 minutes? _____

4.

What time does the clock show? _____

What time would it be if it were 9 hours earlier? _____

What time will it be in 9 hours and 6 minutes? _____

What time will it be in 3 hours and 47 minutes? _____

Helping at Home

Ask your child to estimate how long it takes him or her to get ready for school in the morning. Include eating breakfast, brushing teeth, etc. Have your child draw a clock that shows what time he or she usually does each step.

Word Problems: Time

Answer each question.

1. Isabella wants to watch a show at 8:00 pm. It is 7:23 pm. How many minutes does she have to wait before the show starts?

_____

2. Cade's favorite show starts at 7:30 pm. It is 90 minutes long. What time will the show end?

_____

3. Taylor's favorite show started at 4:30 pm. It is 30 minutes long. It is now 4:53 pm. In how many minutes does the show end?

_____

4. Monique watched a movie that started at 7:00 pm. It lasted 1 hour and 47 minutes. What time did the movie end?

_____

5. Jonathan started watching a show at 4:16 pm. He turned the TV off at 5:37 pm. How long did he watch TV?

_____

6. Chelsea watched two 30-minute shows on Monday, one 30-minute show on Wednesday, and three 30-minute shows on Friday. How many hours of TV did she watch that week?

_____

Ask your child to write down the time he or she starts watching TV each day and the time when the TV is turned off. Then, have your child calculate how long he or she was watching.

Capacity

Capacity is the amount a container can hold when it is full.

1 liter (L) =

1 milliliter (mL) =

Choose the best unit to measure each item.

1. The capacity of a bathtub
   A. L   B. mL

2. The amount of juice in a juice box
   A. L   B. mL

3. The capacity of a canned soft drink
   A. L   B. mL

4. The amount of water in a large bucket
   A. L   B. mL

5. The amount of oil in a teaspoon
   A. L   B. mL

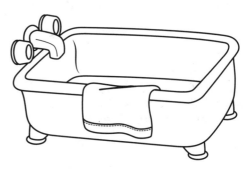

6. One swimming pool can hold 58 L of water, while another can hold 73 L. What is the difference?

   _____

7. Mom bought 12 L of apple juice for the party. Dad bought 9 L more. How many liters did they buy in all?

   _____

8. At the snack counter, 1 cup can hold 215 mL of water. How much water can 3 cups hold?

   _____

9. Suzy had 10 L of water. She wanted to pour an equal amount of water into 5 thermoses. How many liters did she pour into each thermos?

   _____

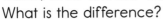

Helping at Home

Give your child a hands-on experience measuring capacity. Allow your child to fill measuring cups with water, then redistribute the water into smaller measuring cups. Discuss other liquids that would be measured in liters or milliliters.

Mass

Mass is the amount of matter in an object.

1 gram (g) =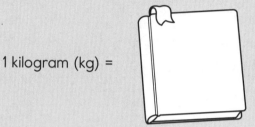

1 kilogram (kg) =

Choose the best unit to measure each item.

1. The mass of a strawberry
    A. g   B. kg

2. The mass of a full suitcase
    A. g   B. kg

3. The amount of matter in a bowling ball
    A. g   B. kg

4. The amount of matter in a pushpin
    A. g   B. kg

5. The mass of an apple
    A. g   B. kg

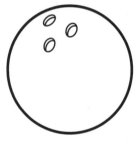

6. Jawan put some apples in a bowl. Each apple had a mass of 200 g. The total mass of all of the apples was 800 g. How many apples were in the bowl?

_____

7. The computer's mass was 5 kg, and the printer's mass was 2 kg. How much mass did they have in all?

_____

8. The moped weighed 15 kg, while the bike weighed 3 kg. How much more mass did the moped have than the bike?

_____

9. Which object probably has more mass: a baseball or a golf ball? Explain.

_____

© Carson-Dellosa • CD-704503

Helping at Home

Give your child two stacks of different colored self-sticking notes, one for grams and one for kilograms. Have your child decide which unit would best measure the mass of different objects around the house and stick the correct note to it.

Bar Graphs

Bar graphs can be used to display and compare information. The bar graph below shows the results of a science experiment to find the best plant food.

Use the bar graph to answer each question.

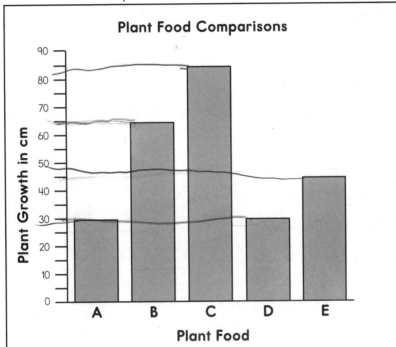

1. How much did the plant that received food B grow? _65 cm long_

2. Which two plant foods produced the same growth? _A_ and _D_

3. How much more did the plant that received food C grow than the plant that received food A?
   50 cm more long

4. How much did the plant that received food E grow? _45 cm long_

5. Which two plant foods produced 110 cm of growth altogether? _A_ and _C_

6. How much more did the plant that received food B grow than the plant that received food D? plant B/ 35 more votes than plant D

Have your child survey friends and family members to find out their favorite ice cream flavors. Encourage your child to carefully record the results. Then, have your child make a bar graph based on the data and display it in your home.

Pictographs

Pictographs use pictures to display and compare information. The pictograph below shows the results of a food drive at Lindy Elementary School.

Use the pictograph to answer each question.

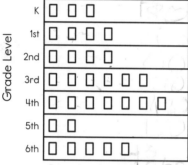

Lindy Elementary Food Drive

Each ☐ stands for 60 pounds of donated food.

1. Which grade level donated the most pounds of food? _____4th grade_____

2. Which grade level donated 120 pounds of food? ___7th grade_____

3. What was the total amount of food donated by the entire school?
_____

4. How many more pounds of food did grade 4 donate than grade 5?
_____

5. Who donated more food, grade 1 or grade 6? _____

6. How many more pounds of food did grade K donate than grade 5?
_____

7. Which grade level donated a total of 300 pounds of food? ___6th Grade_____

8. How many pounds of food did grades 3 and 4 donate altogether?
_____

Helping at Home

© Carson-Dellosa • CD-704503

Measurement: Inches

Measure to the nearest quarter inch.

1.

2.
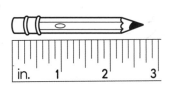

3.

4.
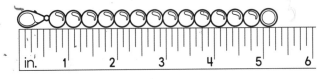

5.

6.

7.

8.
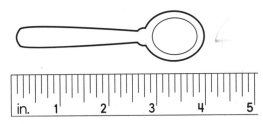

9.
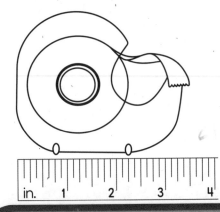

10.

To-do List
- clean

Helping at Home

Give your child five different objects to measure. First, ask your child to estimate the length of each object in inches. Then, have him or her measure it with a ruler and record the actual length to the nearest quarter inch.

Measurement: Inches

Use a ruler to measure to the nearest quarter inch.

1. 	2.	3. 
4.	5.	6. 
7. 	8. 	9.

10. Use the measurements to complete the line plot.

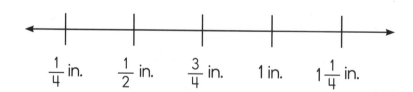

$\frac{1}{4}$ in. $\frac{1}{2}$ in. $\frac{3}{4}$ in.   1 in. $1\frac{1}{4}$ in.

11. Which measurements occurred most frequently? _____

12. Which measurement occurred least frequently? _____

13. How many more objects measured 1 in. than $\frac{1}{4}$ in.? _____

14. How many objects did you measure in all? _____

Helping at Home

Encourage your child to make a line plot to display the five measurements from the Helping at Home activity on page 109. Ask your child if he or she thinks the line plot makes the data easier to read.

Area

Area is the number of square units inside a figure. To find the area, count the number of squares it takes to cover the figure.

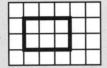

Six squares are inside the figure, so the area is 6 square units

Area = 6 square units

Count the squares to find the area of each figure.

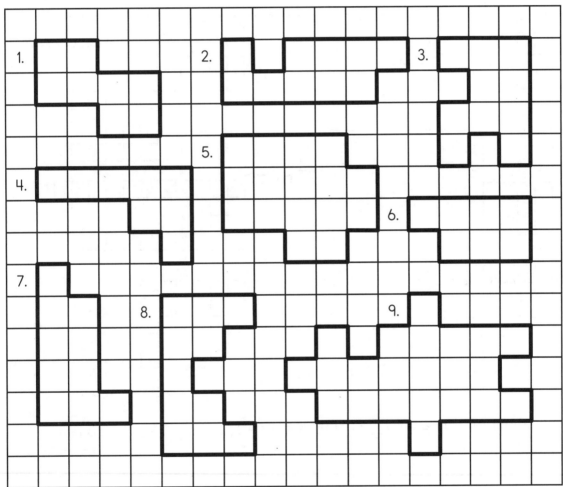

1. Area = _____ cm²

2. Area = _____ cm²

3. Area = _____ cm²

4. Area = _____ cm²

5. Area = _____ cm²

6. Area = _____ cm²

7. Area = _____ cm²

8. Area = _____ cm²

9. Area = _____ cm²

Helping at Home

Provide graph paper with large squares. Encourage your child to use the paper to draw shapes of different sizes. Then, have your child count the square units in each shape and write its area in square units.

Area

When drawing square units to find the area,   □ = 1 square unit
- there should be no gaps;
- there should be no overlapping.   = 9 square units

Find the area.

1. _____

2. _____

3. _____

4. _____

5. _____

6. _____

Draw each number of square units. Then, find the area.

4 units

4 units

6 units

2 units

3 units

5 units

7. _____

8. _____

9. _____

Ask your child to draw a floor plan for his or her dream bedroom on graph paper. Considering each square on the paper to represent 1 ft.^{2}, have your child calculate the area of the room in square feet.

Area

Area is the number of square units enclosed within a boundary. To find the area of a square or a rectangle, draw square units or multiply the length by the width.

4 cm
3 cm

Area = Length x Width
A = 4 cm x 3 cm
A = 12 cm^2

or

4 cm
3 cm

Find the area of each item.

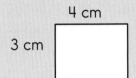

12 in.

6 in.

1. A = _____ in.^{2}

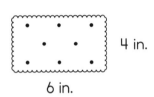

4 in.

6 in.

2. A = _____ in.^{2}

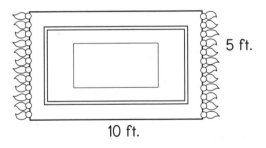

5 ft.

10 ft.

3. A = _____ ft.^{2}

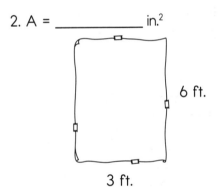

6 ft.

3 ft.

4. A = _____ ft.^{2}

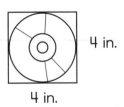

4 in.

4 in.

5. A = _____ in.^{2}

8 in.

10 in.

6. A = _____ in.^{2}

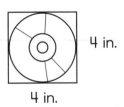

Helping at Home

Ask your child to use a ruler, yardstick, or measuring tape to measure the lengths and widths of objects around your house such as books, rugs, and tabletops. Have your child multiply to find the area of each object in square inches.

Area

When given a large area to calculate, you can break it into smaller sections and then use the formula (a × b) + (a × c).

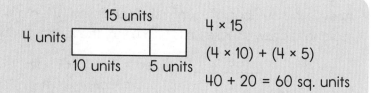

4 × 15

(4 × 10) + (4 × 5)

40 + 20 = 60 sq. units

Find the area.

1.

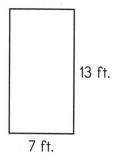

13 ft.

7 ft.

2.

5 m

20 m

3.

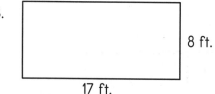

8 ft.

17 ft.

4.

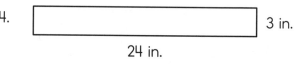

3 in.

24 in.

You can also break apart unusual shapes to find the total area.

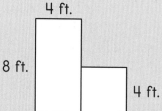

4 ft.

8 ft.

4 ft.

(8 × 4) + (4 × 4)

32 + 16 = 48 sq. ft.

5.

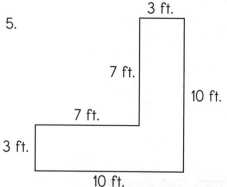

3 ft.

7 ft.

10 ft.

7 ft.

3 ft.

10 ft.

6.

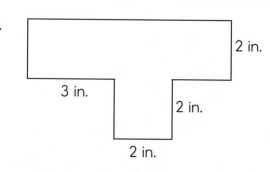

2 in.

3 in.

2 in.

2 in.

Perimeter

Perimeter is the total distance around a figure. To find the perimeter, add the lengths of all of the sides.

8 cm

2 cm

P = 8 cm + 2 cm + 8 cm + 2 cm

P = 20 cm

Label the missing sides. Then, find the perimeter of each figure.

1.

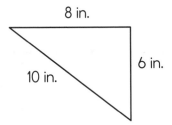

8 cm

4 cm

5 cm

7 cm

P = _____ cm

2.

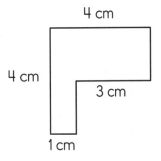

2 ft.

2 ft.

1 ft.

3 ft.

P = _____ ft.

3.

8 in.

6 in.

10 in.

P = _____ in.

4.

4 cm

4 cm

3 cm

1 cm

P = _____ cm

5.

7 yd.

7 yd.

P = _____ yd.

6.

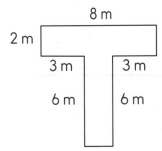

8 m

2 m

3 m   3 m

6 m   6 m

P = _____ m

Helping at Home

Describe a shape to your child and have him or her draw it and find its perimeter. For instance, say, "I'm thinking of a polygon with 5 sides that measure 4 feet each. What is the perimeter?"

Area and Perimeter

Use the diagram to answer each question.

1. What is the area of Kenny's desk? _____

   What is the perimeter? _____

2. What is the area of the fish tank? _____

   What is the perimeter? _____

3. What is the area of the closet? _____

   What is the perimeter? _____

4. What is the area of the computer center? _____

   What is the perimeter? _____

5. How many square feet do the closet and the bookcase total? _____

6. How much larger is the perimeter of Kenny's desk than Amy's desk? _____

Mrs. April's Classroom
(all measurements shown in feet)

	4		2
Computer Center (5)	Closet (3)
Work Table (2, 5)	Amy's Desk (4, 3)	Kenny's Desk (5, 3)
Art Corner (5)	Bookcase (2)	Fish Tank (2)
4	5	3

Polygons

When three or more line segments come together, they form a **polygon**.

A polygon with 3 sides is a **triangle.**

A polygon with 4 sides is a **quadrilateral.**

A polygon with 5 sides is a **pentagon**.

Identify each figure as a triangle, quadrilateral, or pentagon.

1.

_____

2.

_____

3.

_____

4.

_____

5.

_____

6.

_____

7.

_____

8.

_____

9.

_____

10.

_____

11.

_____

12.

_____

Use your finger to trace shapes on your child's back. Have him or her guess if it is a triangle, quadrilateral, or pentagon based on the number of sides. Ask your child to draw shapes on your back, too.

Quadrilaterals

Parallel lines run side by side and never cross.
A **quadrilateral** is any shape with four sides.

Use the shapes to answer the questions.

square   rectangle   trapezoid   rhombus   circle

triangle   pentagon   hexagon   octagon

1. Name the shapes that are quadrilaterals.

   _____   _____

   _____   _____

2. What is the only quadrilateral with four equal sides? _____

3. What shape has three sides and three angles? _____

4. What shape has no sides? _____

5. What shape has five sides? _____

6. What shape has six sides?_____

7. What shape has eight sides? _____

8. What shapes have one set or more of parallel sides?

   _____   _____

   _____   _____

   _____   _____

Helping at Home

Help your child cut the shapes shown on this page from construction paper. Then, ask your child to think of different ways to sort the shapes. Suggest sorting by number of sides, number of angles, whether or not sides are parallel, etc.

Polygons

A **polygon** is a closed plane figure formed by three or more line segments with two sides meeting at each vertex.

| parallelogram | quadrilateral | square | rectangle | rhombus | trapezoid |

Identify each figure.

1.

_____

2.

_____

3.

_____

4.

_____

5.

_____

6.

_____

7.

_____

8.

_____

9.

_____

10.

_____

11. What do shapes 1 to 10 have in common?

_____

_____

Draw each shape.

12. rhombus

13. rectangle

14. square

Equal Parts

Cross out the shapes that are not divided equally. Label how each remaining shape is divided.

1. A.   B.    C. 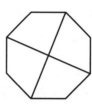   D.

_____   _____   _____   _____

2. A.   B. 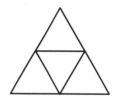   C. 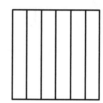   D.

_____   _____   _____   _____

Divide each shape.

3. A. 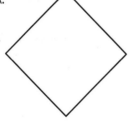   B.    C. 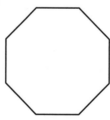   D.

   eighths   halves   eighths   tenths

4. A. 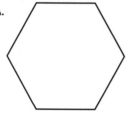   B.    C.    D.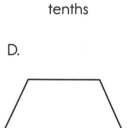

   sixths   thirds   fourths   thirds

Make a homemade pizza with your child. Allow him or her to cut the pizza into equal pieces. Discuss how many people the pizza must serve and let your child decide how to divide the pizza.

Partitioning Shapes

 To **partition** a shape means to divide it. When showing fractions, partition shapes into equal parts.

Connect the dots to form different geometric shapes. Then, divide them into equal parts.

1.

Connect the dots to form a triangle.
Divide it into fourths.

2.

Connect the dots to form a square.
Divide it into fifths.

3.

Connect the dots to form a trapezoid.
Divide it into halves.

4.

Connect the dots to form a rhombus.
Divide it into thirds.

 Helping at Home Draw more dots on a piece of paper. Take turns with your child, connecting two dots at a time to form shapes. When a player completes a shape, the other player gets to decide how many equal parts it should be divided into.

Answer Key

Page 11

1. C; 2. A; 3. Answers will vary. 4. Answers will vary, but should include the idea of ordinary. 5. A

Page 13

1. A; 2. Answers will vary. 3. A. people, animals, food, rides; B. animals, barkers; C. animals; hot dogs, cotton candy; D. animals, food; E. hot dogs, cotton candy, drinks; 4. A; 5. air, Answers will vary. 6. fed, Answers will vary. 7. fly, Answers will vary. 8. today, Answers will vary.

Page 15

1. A; 2. 5, 1, 2, 4, 3; 3. A; 4. pulling my leg/teasing me, hit the road/go or leave, talk my ear off/talk too much, shoot the breeze/talk about nothing in particular, time flew/time passed quickly; 5. begged; 6. logging

Page 17

1. Heroes choose to act selflessly. Heroes give it their all. Heroes keep trying. Heroes go the extra mile. 2. A; 3. Answers will vary. 4. B; 5. B

Page 19

1. B; 2. F, T, T, T; 3. B; 4. C; 5. A. k, gh; B. e; C. k, w; D. e; E. k, c; F. e; 6. their; 7. his

Page 21

1. B; 2. T, F, F, T, T; 3. A; 4. A. milk; B. candy bar; C. cheese; 5. Answers will vary. 6. A. Grains; B. Dairy

Page 23

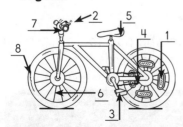

Page 25

1. at the pet shop; 2. Grandma hasn't seen Poochy since she stopped at that shop. 3. B; 4. 3, 2, 1, 4

Page 27

1. A; 2. Franklin wrote books and newspaper articles. He helped write the Declaration of Independence. He discovered new facts about electricity. 3. 5, 4, 2, 1, 3; 4. Answers will vary. 5. inventor; 6. printer; 7. writer; 8. helper; 9. Franklin invented a type of glasses because he wanted to be able to read in his old age. 10. Franklin helped start the first fire station after a fire destroyed much of Philadelphia. 11. Franklin is still an American hero today, although he died on April 17, 1790.

Page 28

1. stream, middle of the stream; 2. view, view before; 3. test, after the test; 4. charge, charge again; 5. color, one color or single color; 6. scope, scope used to see very small things; 7. zero, below zero; 8. fiction, not fiction; 9. nonliving; 10. unicycle; 11. microchip; 12. preheat; 13. submarine; 14. reattach

Page 29

1. -ation, educate, Answers will vary. 2. -ment, treat, Answers will vary. 3. -ify, glory, Answers will vary. 4. -ty, cruel, Answers will vary. 5. -ible, collapse, Answers will vary. 6. -ation, salute, Answers will vary. 7. -able, wash, Answers will vary. 8. -ify, notice, Answers will vary.

9. If you don't know how to stop, you might crash. 10. You might be hit by a car if you don't signal to let others know where you are going. 11. You might lose control of your bike and fall or crash. 12. B; 13. B; 14. A; 15. B; 16. B; 17. Answers will vary.

Answer Key

Page 30

1. plant, to plant across; 2. help, full of help; 3. work, one who works; 4. grown, too much growth; 5. understand, understand wrongly; 6. hope, without hope; 7. thankful; 8. painless; 9. overspend; 10. teacher; 11. transport; 12. misspell

Page 31

ba/con, 2; ba/gels, 2; be/gins, 2; co/coa, 2; ci/der, 2; de/lic/ious, 3; ex/ci/ted, 3; fi/nal, 2; fla/vors, 2; li/lacs, 2; mu/sic, 2; na/vy, 2; pho/to/graphs, 3; re/mem/ber, 3; re/sist, 2; si/lent, 2; ta/ble, 2; ti/dy, 2; She will fry <u>bacon</u> and sausage. Some of her friends like bread and others like <u>bagels</u>. She bought jelly and two different <u>flavors</u> of cream cheese. Lucy will serve apple <u>cider</u> and hot <u>cocoa</u>. Lucy is <u>excited</u> to decorate the <u>table</u>. She bought a <u>navy</u>-and-white striped tablecloth. Then, she filled baskets with <u>lilacs</u> and ivy. The <u>final</u> thing she does is choose peaceful <u>music</u>. She doesn't want a <u>silent</u> party. Lucy can't <u>resist</u> piano tunes so she downloads several songs. When Lucy's guests arrive, she <u>begins</u> to serve the food. She takes <u>photographs</u> so she will <u>remember</u> the event. As her guests finish eating, they help her <u>tidy</u> up the kitchen. Everyone thanks Lucy for a <u>delicious</u> breakfast party.

Page 32

af/ter, 2; an/i/mals, 3; broc/co/li, 3; car/rots, 2; cir/cles, 2; com/pu/ters, 3; e/lec/tri/ci/ty, 5; en/joy, 2; fol/low, 2; gal/ax/y, 3; hab/it, 2; ham/ster, 2; let/tuce, 2; li/brar/y, 3; pen/cils, 2; pic/tures, 2; plan/e/tar/i/um, 5; plan/ets, 2; play/ful, 2; sys/tem, 2; top/ics, 2; Our class studies many interesting <u>topics.</u> My favorite unit was about <u>planets.</u> I drew <u>pictures</u> of the solar <u>system.</u> Next week, we are going to the <u>planetarium.</u> We will learn about constellations and our <u>galaxy.</u> I also love learning about <u>animals.</u> We have a class <u>hamster.</u> We take turns feeding him fresh vegetables like <u>broccoli</u> and <u>carrots</u> (or <u>lettuce</u>). Sometimes, he eats <u>lettuce</u> (or <u>carrots</u>), too. Our hamster is very <u>playful</u>! He likes to <u>follow</u> his tail around and run in <u>circles.</u> He also has a <u>habit</u> of scratching his nose. <u>After</u> school, my friends and I help our teacher. I sharpen the <u>pencils.</u> My friends tidy up our classroom <u>library.</u> We turn off all of the <u>computers</u> and the lights to save <u>electricity.</u> We <u>enjoy</u> helping our teacher.

Page 33

1. Astronomy; 2. especially; 3. telescope; 4. conditions; 5. observations; 6. constellations; 7. compass

Page 34

1. range; 2. scarce; 3. natives; 4. dependent; 5. stalked; 6. accuracy; 7. conceal; 8. migrated

Page 35

1. atmosphere; 2. launched; 3. evaluated; 4. mission; 5. transformed; 6. distort; 7. former; 8. theories; 9. universe; 10. payloads

Page 36

Answers will vary.

Page 37

Answers will vary.

Page 38

Answers will vary.

Page 39

Answers will vary.

Page 40

Answers will vary.

Page 41

Answers will vary.

Page 42

Answers will vary but may include: <u>First</u>, I have to take a warm shower. <u>Next</u>, I put on my clothes. <u>Then</u>, I have to make my bed. <u>Now</u>, I have to wake my little brother. <u>First</u>, I whisper his name. <u>Next</u>, I give him a gentle push. <u>Eventually</u>, my stomach starts growling. I <u>then</u> brush my teeth and comb my hair. I can <u>finally</u>

Answer Key

head off to school!

Page 43

Answers will vary.

Page 44

Answers will vary.

Page 45

Answers will vary.

Page 46

Answers will vary.

Page 47

Answers will vary.

Page 48

Answers will vary.

Page 49

1. linking; 2. action; 3. action; 4. action; 5. linking; 6. action; 7. action; 8. action; 9. action; 10. linking; 11. begins; 12. sell; 13. gather; 14. explodes; 15. dash; 16. rain; 17. escape; 18. cover

Page 50

1. gentle, friendly; 2. big, beautiful; 3. split, upper; 4. thick, wool; 5. soft; 6. smart; 7. long; 8. sure-footed; 9. wonderful, pack; 10. two-toed

Page 51

1. how, bravely (circled), fought (underlined); 2. how, foolishly (circled), chased (underlined); 3. where, downstairs (circled), walked (underlined); 4. when,

today (circled), played (underlined); 5. where, somewhere (circled), lost (underlined); 6. where, away (circled), sailed (underlined); 7. how, honestly (circled), played (underlined); 8. how, carefully (circled), fed (underlined); 9. when, tomorrow (circled), coming (underlined); 10. where, outside (circled), planted (underlined); 11-14. Answers will vary.

Page 52

1. louder, loudest; 2. slower, slowest; 3. faster, fastest; 4. more closely, most closely; 5. more calmly, most calmly; 6. more quietly, most quietly; 7. more smoothly, most smoothly; 8. more softly, most softly; 9. suddenly; 10. faster; 11. warmly

Page 53

1. him; 2. them; 3. her; 4. it; 5. it; 6. us; 7. it; 8. them; 9. us; 10. it; 11. them; 12. her; 13. it; 14. them; 15. it

Page 54

1. C; 2. C; 3. C; 4. P; 5. S; 6. S; 7. S; 8. C; 9. C; 10. C; 11. P; 12. C; 13. P; 14. S; 15. C; 16. litter; 17. swarm; 18. gaggle; 19. plague; 20. pod; 21. school; 22. herd; 23. pack; 24. Answers will vary.

Page 55

Person: bride, maiden, infant, orphan, partner, bachelor; **Place:** pharmacy, mansion, studio, lobby, university, fortress; **Thing:**

awning, hexagon, table, souvenir, satellite, cabinet; 1. abstract; 2. abstract; 3. concrete; 4. abstract; 5. concrete; 6. abstract; 7. Answers will vary.

Page 56

1. delayed; 2. helped; 3. placed; 4. arrived; 5. slipped; 6. trimmed; 7. magnified; 8. propelled; 9. looked; 10. wanted; 11. applied; 12. carried; 13. supplied

Page 57

1. shot; 2. taught; 3. drew; 4. found; 5. spoke; 6. felt; 7. held; 8. wrote; 9. heard; 10. caught; 11. I saw a monarch butterfly on a milkweed plant. 12. The butterfly made its egg sticky. 13. The tiny white egg stuck to the leaf. 14. A small caterpillar came out of the egg.

Page 58

1. longer, longest; 2. broader, broadest; 3. larger, largest; 4. flatter, flattest; 5. sweeter, sweetest; 6. wider, widest; 7. cooler, coolest; 8. smarter, smartest

Page 59

1. and; 2. but; 3. and; 4. or; 5. and; 6. but; 7. but; 8. and; 9. and; 10. or

Page 60

1. "Are you ready to leave?" Grandpa asked. 2. "I had a huge breakfast this morning," Miguel said. 3. Libby said, "Wait for me! I

Answer Key

don't want to be late." 4. "I stubbed my toe on the way to the bus stop," Jack moaned. 5. "Hooray! I won the race!" Riley exclaimed. 6. "Would you like a slice of apple pie?" Mrs. Havel asked. 7. Ryan said, "I would like to go for a swim." 8. Parker replied, "No, I have not seen your lunch box."

Page 61

1. use; 2. propels; 3. are; 4. dig; 5. carries; 6. enjoy; 7. steers; 8. is; 9. are; 10. pulls; 11. do; 12. fish; 13. race

Page 62

1. teachers'; 2. teeth's; 3. bracelet's; 4. galaxy's; 5. men's; 6. T. rex's; 7. Tess's; 8. children's; 9. industries'; 10. students'; 11. meadow's; 12. tennis's; 13. Tuesday's; 14. countesses'; 15. the french fries' flavor; 16. Canada's economy; 17. the crowd's cheers; 18. the pies' aroma

Page 63

1. team; 2. quarterback; 3. passed; 4. sprinted; 5. Fans; 6. referee; 7. Bobcats; 8. coaches; 9. returned; 10. quarterback; 11. tied; 12. stands

Page 68

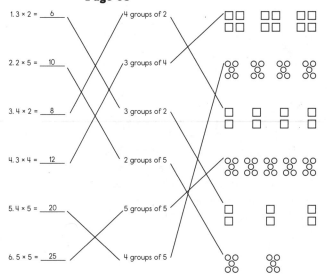

1. 3 × 2 = 6
2. 2 × 5 = 10
3. 4 × 2 = 8
4. 3 × 4 = 12
5. 4 × 5 = 20
6. 5 × 5 = 25

7. 16, Drawings will vary. 8. 9, Drawings will vary.

Page 69

Answers will vary.

Page 70

1. 7, Drawings will vary. 21 – 3 = 18, 18 – 3 = 15, 15 – 3 = 12, 12 – 3 = 9, 9 – 3 = 6, 6 – 3 = 3, 3 – 3 = 0; 2. 6, Drawings will vary. 30 – 5 = 25, 25 – 5 = 20, 20 – 5 = 15, 15 – 5 = 10, 10 – 5 = 5, 5 – 5 = 0; 3. 4, Drawings will vary. 36 – 9 = 27, 27 – 9 = 18, 18 – 9 = 9, 9 – 9 = 0; 4. 3, Drawings will vary. 18 – 6 = 12, 12 – 6 = 6, 6 – 6 = 0

Page 71

Answers will vary.

Page 72

1. 54 marbles; 2. 32 cards; 3. 45 times; 4. 30 miles; 5. 28 skaters; 6. 48 bandages

Page 73

1. 81 boxes; 2. 56 students; 3. 42 pictures; 4. 72 cards; 5. 14 pages; 6. 40 marbles

Page 74

1. 9, 6, 10, 3; 2. 7, 9, 7, 4; 3. 9, 3, 9, 4; 4. 8, 8, 9, 10; 5. 7, 4, 5, 7; 6. 6, 6, 9; 7. 42, 45, 28; 8. 80, 7, 9; 9. 3, 30, 30; 10. 2, 49, 8

Page 75

1.

Rule: × 2	
2	14
3	6
4	8
5	10
6	12
7	14

2.

Rule: ÷ 3	
12	4
21	7
30	10
15	5
60	20
24	8

3.

Rule: × 5	
2	10
3	15
4	20
5	25
6	30
7	35

4.

Rule: ÷ 4	
2	10
3	8
4	1
5	11
6	9
7	7

5. × 4; 6. ÷ 5

Answer Key

Page 76

1. $2 \times 4 = 8$, $4 \times 2 = 8$; 2. $2 \times 6 = 12$, $6 \times 2 = 12$; 3. $3 \times 4 = 12$, $4 \times 3 = 12$; 4. $3 \times 5 = 15$, $5 \times 3 = 15$; 5. $2 \times 5 = 10$, $5 \times 2 = 10$; 6. $4 \times 5 = 20$, $5 \times 4 = 20$; 7. 24; 8. 30; 9. 14; 10. 16; 11. 24; 12. 18; 13. 8; 14. 5; 15. 2; 16. 3

Page 77

1. $(2 \times 6) \times 1 = 12$, $2 \times (6 \times 1) = 12$; 2. $(9 \times 10) \times 1 = 90$, $9 \times (10 \times 1) = 90$; 3. $(7 \times 4) \times 3 = 84$, $7 \times (4 \times 3) = 84$; 4. $(8 \times 3) \times 2 = 48$, $8 \times (3 \times 2) = 48$; 5. $(10 \times 5) \times 4 = 200$, $10 \times (5 \times 4) = 200$; 6. $(3 \times 4) \times 2 = 24$, $3 \times (4 \times 2) = 24$; 7. $(4 \times 2) \times 5 = 40$, $4 \times (2 \times 5) = 40$; 8. $(2 \times 10) \times 3 = 60$, $2 \times (10 \times 3) = 60$

Page 78

1. 56; 2. 51; 3. 110; 4. 72; 5. 78; 6. 84

Page 79

1. 6; 2. 1; 3. 5; 4. 8; 5. 7; 6. 9; 7. 10; 8. 2; 9. 4; 10. 3; A SWIFTWALKER

Page 80

1. 30, 49, 27, 32; 2. 45, 18, 42, 45; 3. 81, 24, 21, 36; 4. 56, 54, 36, 64; 5. 8, 60, 15, 18, 55, 28, 24; 6. 6, 35, 18, 24, 32, 10, 27; 7. 16, 9, 45, 12, 42, 30, 48; 8. 36, 63, 56, 40, 36, 32, 49; 9. 25, 28, 72, 14

Page 81

1. 3, 2; 2. 4, 3; 3. 3, 5; 4. 2, 5; 5. 8, 2; 6. 5, 4; 7. 4, 6; 8. 7, 4; 9. 4, 9; 10. 2, 8; 11. 8, 6; 12. 6, 9; 13. 8; 14. 7; 15. 9; 16. 8; 17. 7; 18. 7; 19. 4; 20. 5; 21. 9; 22. 8; 23. 8; 24. 4

Page 82

1. Yes. The total of the two items is $3.48. 2. Yes, he will get $1.53 in change. 3. No, he does not. Six quarters equals $1.50. He needs $1.99 for a pineapple. 4. She bought grapes.

Page 83

1. 10 sundaes; 2. 8 bones; 3. 14 more apples; 4. 21 games; 5. 4 walnuts; 6. 3 cookies each, 3 left over

Page 84

1. 40; 2. 60; 3. 60; 4. 90; 5. 70; 6. 30; 7. 30; 8. 40; 9. 20; 10. 40; 11. 300; 12. 990; 13. 460; 14. 430; 15. 690; 16. 920; 17. 780; 18. 380; 19. 250; 20. 720; 21. about 40 nuts; 22. about 20 more stamps

Page 85

1. $700; 2. $100; 3. $600; 4. $300; 5. $700; 6. $900; 7. $700; 8. $500; 9. $900

Page 86

1. 49, 59, 98, 89, 96, 49; 2. 73, 87, 27, 68, 95, 57; 3. 54, 40, 22, 65, 61, 15; 4. 26, 20, 24, 23, 51, 50; 5. 885, 778, 988, 998, 527; 6. 594, 986, 969, 789, 919; 7. 431, 213, 225, 236, 223

Page 87

1. 51, 92, 81, 86, 64, 90; 2. 94, 130, 92, 92, 103, 102; 3. 19, 79, 19, 26, 16, 49; 4. 19, 58, 14, 59, 28, 32; 5. 940, 610, 1,091, 1,311, 420; 6. 611, 613, 617, 1,211, 1,059; 7. 699, 269, 469, 429, 257

Page 88

1. 80, 70, 40, 90, 30; 2. 60, 100, 20, 50, 30; 3. 40, 420, 60, 240, 810; 4. 400, 120, 560, 300, 200

Page 89

1. ; 2. $\frac{1}{4}$; 3. ; 4. $\frac{1}{3}$; 5. $\frac{1}{6}$; 6. ; 7. Wyatt is correct because the shape is not divided into three equal pieces. 8. Yes, he did. While the shapes are different, they are both divided into four equal pieces, and both have three of the four sections shaded.

Answer Key

Page 90

1. $\frac{1}{6}$; 2. $\frac{3}{8}$; 3. $\frac{1}{2}$; 4. $\frac{5}{8}$; 5. $\frac{10}{16}$; 6. $\frac{7}{12}$

Page 91

1. $\frac{1}{2}$; 2. $\frac{1}{4}$; 3. $\frac{2}{4}$ or $\frac{1}{2}$; 4. $\frac{3}{4}$; 5. $\frac{1}{8}$; 6. $\frac{2}{8}$ or $\frac{1}{4}$; 7. $\frac{3}{8}$; 8. $\frac{4}{8}$, $\frac{2}{4}$, or $\frac{1}{2}$; 9. $\frac{5}{8}$; 10. $\frac{6}{8}$ or $\frac{3}{4}$; 11. $\frac{7}{8}$

Page 93

1. number line
2. number line
3. number line

Page 95

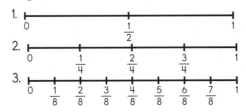

1. $\frac{1}{6}$ $\frac{2}{3}$; 2. $\frac{3}{6}$ $\frac{4}{6}$ $\frac{5}{6}$; 3. $\frac{3}{8}$ $\frac{4}{8}$; 4. $\frac{1}{3}$ $\frac{2}{3}$;
5. number line
6. number line
7. Answers will vary.

Page 96

1. $\frac{1}{3} = \frac{2}{6}$; 2. $\frac{1}{4} = \frac{2}{8}$; 3. $\frac{1}{2} = \frac{3}{6}$; 4. $\frac{3}{4} = \frac{6}{8}$; 5. $\frac{2}{2} = \frac{1}{1}$ or 1; 6. $\frac{3}{7} = \frac{6}{14}$; 7. $\frac{1}{5} = \frac{2}{10}$; 8. $\frac{1}{6} = \frac{2}{12}$; 9. $\frac{8}{8} = \frac{1}{1}$ or 1; 10. $\frac{2}{3} = \frac{6}{9}$; 11. $\frac{2}{4} = \frac{8}{16}$; 12. $\frac{1}{4} = \frac{3}{12}$

Page 97

1. 2; 2. 2; 3. 4; 4. 8; 5. 4; 6. 2; 7. 2; 8. 2, 6, 4

Page 98

1. The fractions $\frac{2}{4}$ and $\frac{1}{2}$ are equivalent because they both fall on the same spot on the number line. ;
2. number line
3. $\frac{1}{4} = \frac{2}{8}$, $\frac{2}{4} = \frac{4}{8}$, $\frac{3}{4} = \frac{6}{8}$; 4. Answers will vary but may include $\frac{2}{2}$, $\frac{3}{3}$, $\frac{4}{4}$, $\frac{5}{5}$, $\frac{6}{6}$, $\frac{7}{7}$, or $\frac{8}{8}$. They are equivalent because on a number line

they all fall on the same spot.
5. They are not equivalent because $\frac{5}{8}$ is greater than $\frac{1}{2}$. 6. Answers will vary.

Page 99

1. $\frac{12}{3}$; 2. $\frac{4}{2}$; 3. $\frac{12}{6}$; 4. $\frac{20}{4}$; 5. $\frac{10}{2}$; 6. $\frac{24}{6}$; 7. $\frac{3}{1}$; 8. $\frac{4}{1}$; 9. $\frac{2}{1}$; 10–15. Answers will vary.

Page 100

1. 4; 2. 5; 3. 4; 4. 6; 5. 2; 6. 5; 7. 7; 8. 7; 9. 8; 10. 9; 11. 3; 12. 5; 13. 11; 14. 10

Page 101

1. $\frac{1}{3} < \frac{2}{3}$; 2. $\frac{2}{4} = \frac{4}{8}$; 3. $\frac{3}{8} < \frac{1}{2}$; 4. $\frac{1}{3} = \frac{2}{6}$; 5. $\frac{3}{4} > \frac{2}{4}$;
6. $\frac{1}{2} < \frac{3}{4}$

Page 102

1. <; 2. <; 3. >; 4. <; 5. >; 6. > 7. If the denominators are the same, the fraction with the smaller numerator is smaller. 8. >; 9. <; 10. <; 11. <; 12. >; 13. >; 14. If the numerators are the same, the fraction with the smaller denominator is greater.

Page 103

1. 8:00, 7:40, 11:35, 9:05; 2. 1:38, 12:50, 7:00, 2:35; 3. 10:45, 2:30, 3:00, 12:00; 4. 12:25, 3:25, 9:31, 4:12

Page 104

1. 37 minutes; 2. 9:00 pm; 3. 7 minutes; 4. 8:47 pm; 5. 1 hour, 21 minutes; 6. 3 hours

Page 105

1. A. L; 2. B. mL; 3. B. mL; 4. A. L; 5. B. mL; 6. 15 L; 7. 21 L; 8. 645 mL; 9. 2 L

Page 106

1. A. g; 2. B. kg; 3. B. kg; 4. A. g; 5. A. g; 6. 4 apples; 7. 7 kg; 8. 12 kg; 9. baseball, Answers will vary.

Answer Key

Page 107

1. 65 cm; 2. food A, food D;
3. 55 cm; 4. 45 cm; 5. food B, food E; 6. 35 cm

Page 108

1. grade 4; 2. grade 5; 3.
1,860 pounds; 4. 300 pounds;
5. grade 6; 6. 60 pounds; 7.
grade 6; 8. 780 pounds

Page 109

1. $2\frac{1}{2}$ in.; 2. $2\frac{3}{4}$ in.; 3. 1 in.;
4. $5\frac{1}{4}$ in.; 5. 3 in.; 6. $3\frac{1}{2}$ in.;
7. $2\frac{1}{4}$ in.; 8. 4 in. 9. $3\frac{1}{2}$ in.;
10. $1\frac{3}{4}$ in.

Page 110

1. 1 in.; 2. $\frac{1}{2}$ in.; 3. $1\frac{1}{4}$ in.; 4. $\frac{1}{4}$
in.; 5. $\frac{1}{2}$ in.; 6. 1 in.; 7. 1 in.;
8. $1\frac{1}{4}$ in.; 9. $\frac{1}{2}$ in. 11. $\frac{1}{2}$ in. and
1 in.; 12. $\frac{3}{4}$ in.; 13. 2 more; 14. 9

Page 111

1. 8; 2. 10; 3. 10; 4. 8; 5. 16; 6. 7;
7. 10; 8. 11; 9. 22

Page 112

1. 24 sq. units; 2. 40 sq. units;
3. 40 sq. units; 4. 30 sq. units;
5. 51 sq. units; 6. 24 sq. units;

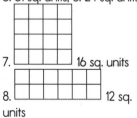

7. 16 sq. units

8. 12 sq. units

Page 113

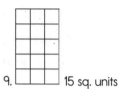

9. 15 sq. units

1. 72; 2. 24; 3. 50; 4. 18; 5. 16;
6. 80

Page 114

1. 91 sq. ft. 2. 100 sq. m; 3. 136
sq. ft. 4. 72 sq. in. 5. 51 sq. ft.
6. 18 sq. in.

Page 115

1. 24; 2. 10; 3. 24; 4. 16; 5. 21;
6. 32

Page 116

1. 15 sq. ft., 16 ft. 2. 6 sq. ft., 10
ft. 3. 6 sq. ft., 10 ft. 4. 20 sq.
ft., 18 ft. 5. 16 sq. ft. 6. 2 feet
larger

Page 117

1. quadrilateral; 2. triangle;
3. triangle; 4. pentagon; 5.
quadrilateral; 6. triangle; 7.
pentagon; 8. pentagon; 9.
quadrilateral; 10. triangle; 11.
quadrilateral; 12. pentagon

Page 118

1. square, rectangle,
trapezoid, rhombus; 2.
square; 3. triangle; 4. circle;
5. pentagon; 6. hexagon;
7. octagon; 8. square,
rectangle, trapezoid,
hexagon, rhombus, octagon

Page 119

1. rhombus; 2. rectangle;
3. quadrilateral; 4.
quadrilateral; 5. square; 6.
parallelogram; 7. rectangle;
8. parallelogram; 9.
quadrilateral; 10. square; 11.
They are all quadrilaterals.
12-14. Check child's drawings.

Page 120

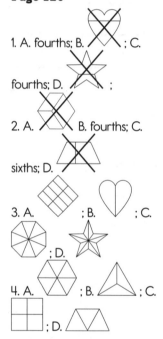

1. A. fourths; B. ; C.
fourths; D. ;
2. A. B. fourths; C.
sixths; D.
3. A. ; B. ; C.
; D.
4. A. ; B. ; C.
; D.

Page 121

1-4. Answers will vary.